The Epistle of Paul to the Philippians

The Epistle of Paul to the Philippians

An Exposition by
Charles R. Erdman

BAKER BOOK HOUSE
Grand Rapids, Michigan 49506

Paperback edition reprinted by Baker Book House
with permission of The Westminster Press

ISBN: 0-8010-3404-3

First printing, November 1983

Printed in the United States of America

PREFACE

The writer of this book on Philippians was "an expositor, an exegete, and a commentator," all in one. He had to have first-hand acquaintanceship with the Greek language, and be well schooled in New Testament disciplines. His task was enormous. Think, for example, of the questions that must be considered on this one New Testament book. Some of these questions are: Who were the Philippians? Who had founded their church, when, and under what circumstances? How was the famous "Macedonian Call" related to this church? Why is Paul believed to be the writer of the letter? Where was Paul in prison when he wrote this letter—Rome, Caesarea, Ephesus? What specific purpose produced the letter? When was it sent, and who carried it to Philippi? How far was Philippi from Rome (important to know if it was the Roman prison from which Paul wrote, because the distance is some 800 miles, and Paul writes of frequent communications between him and the Philippians)? What can be learned about the church in Philippi from The Acts? Who were the "bishops and deacons" mentioned in the salutation? Why was no mention made of Lydia when she figured so prominently in the founding of the church? What parts of the letter are most frequently quoted? What is most unique about this letter in comparison with other Pauline letters? And in addition to all such questions, the "expositor-exegete-commentator" must explain and interpret the entire text composed of approximately 2,100 words. To do justice to his task the writer must be both *objective* and *subjective*. He does not read his own opinions into the text, but interprets the text as a believer who has experienced personally the call of Christ, and who is seeking, as Paul stated to the Philippians, "For to me to live is Christ." God speaks through the Word, but he who hears must be tuned to God.

Dr. Charles R. Erdman was the author of this book on Philippians, as well as the other sixteen volumes in this series. At the time he wrote the book he was professor of practical theology in Princeton Seminary. Previously he had been pastor of two growing churches in Philadelphia, and was continuing a pastorate in the First Presbyterian Church in Princeton while occupying the chair in the seminary. When Dr. Erdman wrote he was picturing the people who would be studying Philippians in the future. Pastors, obviously. Sunday school teachers, certainly. Men, women, and young people in study groups of all kinds. College and seminary students. And a surprising number of lay men and women who order books of this kind for their own personal enrichment. In the past this book, and this series of Erdman New Testament commentaries, has been used until the type and plates have been badly worn—too worn to make additional printings. A completely new set was created to issue this paperback edition. It goes forth as bread cast upon the waters that will not return void.

EARL F. ZEIGLER

FOREWORD

Here is a "hymn of joy." At least the composition is pitched to that high key. The music is the more appealing because its accompaniment sounds the notes of privation and loneliness and poverty and pain. The lines are penned by a prisoner. They are designed to express his gratitude to the friends whose gift has brought relief. More fully do they reveal his conscious relationship to a divine Lord. The service of Christ is the very sphere of his life; the spirit of Christ is the temper of his mind; the perfection of Christ is the goal of his effort; the power of Christ is the secret of his triumph. His artless unfolding of personal experience points every reader to the one pathway of peace and strength and unfailing gladness. Here one can learn to sing songs in the night.

INTRODUCTION

THE CITY OF PHILIPPI

The name of Philippi is famous not so much for its relation to Philip of Macedon as for its connection with the apostle Paul. It is known throughout all the modern world, not because the fate of the Roman republic was sealed by a battle fought outside the city walls, but because a century later a short letter was written by the apostle to a Chrisian church he had established within the city gates.

The original name of the place had been Crenides, or "The Little Fountains," because near it were numerous springs. The region was important because of the rich deposits of gold and silver in the mountains to the south, and further because through a pass in these mountains lay the natural trade routes from the East to the West, from Asia to Europe.

Philip II of Macedonia, the father of Alexander the Great, recognized the strategic value of this region. It lay just beyond the Thracian border. Therefore, in 356 B.C., four years after he took charge of the government of Macedonia, Philip annexed the territory, enlarged and fortified the town, and gave it the name Philippi, "Pertaining to Philip." He worked the mines with such energy that he secured from them more than one thousand talents a year, and found it possible to provide for the West a currency in gold. The vast revenue thus derived enabled Philip not only to enlarge the Macedonian army but to develop the fine art of bribery, in which he is alleged to have been an adept, as evidenced by the statement commonly attributed to him, "that no fortress was impregnable to whose walls an ass laden with gold could be driven." As stated by a certain French writer, "This gold of Crenides spread itself over Greece, preceding the phalanx like an advance guard and opening more gates than the battering-rams and cata-pults."

By the time of the Roman conquest, two centuries later, these rich mines seem to have been exhausted. This conquest was consummated by the Battle of Pydna in 168 B.C. As the result of the victory by the Roman consul, Paulus Aemilius, all the dominions of Perseus, the last king of Macedonia, including Philippi, fell into the hands of Rome and the Province of Macedonia was formally established. By this time, according to the statement of the historian, Strabo, the city of Philippi had so far declined as to be described as "a small settlement."

However, in 42 B.C. Philippi emerged forever from obscurity, for in the autumn of that year it witnessed the famous conflict between the combined forces of Brutus and Cassius and those of Octavian and Mark Antony. The first two leaders had assassinated Julius Caesar with the hope of restoring the republic; of the other two, Octavian subsequently won for himself the position of emperor and assumed the title of Augustus.

The Battle of Philippi consisted of two main engagements. The forces on each side numbered nineteen legions. Cassius had encamped on the slopes of Mt. Pangaeus, to the south of the town, and Brutus on the heights toward the north. In the first engagement Brutus was victorious over Octavian, while Antony defeated Cassius. The forces of Cassius were completely routed, with the loss of eight thousand men, and he himself, believing his cause to be hopeless, compelled his own freedman, Pindarius, to put him to death. Twenty days later the impatient troops of Brutus forced their leader again to join battle. This time he was disastrously defeated and in despair fell on his own sword.

Octavian and Antony had triumphed but it was at the cost of the lives of sixteen thousand of their followers. This conflict, however, determined the course of Roman history and by it the death of Caesar was in large measure avenged. Soon after, Philippi was erected into a colony under the name of "*Colonia Julia Philippensis,*" the very title indicating the triumph of the cause of Julius Caesar.

Eleven years later, after the victory of Octavian over Antony in the Battle of Actium, 31 B.C., the colony was greatly strengthened largely by partisans of Antony, who had been dispossessed of their lands in Italy in order that allotments might be made for the supporters of Octavian. This second foundation of Philippi was commemorated by the additional title of "*Augusta,*" the full name being "*Colonia Augusta Julia (Victrix) Philippensium.*" Coins are still in existence which attest this title.

The fact that Philippi was a colony not only is attested by the historian, but also throws much light on the narratives both of The Acts and of the epistle to the Philippians. It will be remembered that a Roman colony was an outpost, an extension, a small reproduction of the Imperial City. It was in reality a miniature Rome. It possessed many privileges, the chief of which were guaranteed by the coveted statute known to jurists as the *jus Italicum.* This law secured for the colonists freedom and the rights of Roman citizenship, their names still being enrolled among the Roman tribes. Furthermore, they were exempt from taxation and tribute. They also were allowed to hold land in full ownership under the forms of Roman law. The magistrates of each colony were two in number, and in both their civil and military authority they were independent even of the provincial governors in whose territories they were located.

This atmosphere of a Roman colony pervades the story of Philippi as narrated in The Acts as well as in the epistle written by Paul. The magistrates of the city arrogated to themselves the title of "praetors," or commandants. They gave to their attendants, or "serjeants," the title of "lictors." They assumed airs which were appropriate to consuls in imperial Rome. The people in the story of The Acts were easily stirred by a charge against Paul which implied that Roman customs were being imperiled; and, on the other hand, the magistrates were terrified when they learned of their own injustice to a Roman citizen. So, too, when Paul wrote from the imperial capital to residents of a Roman colony he referred to their political privileges to enforce the duties of their Christian profession and he found in their civil liberties the symbol of their citizenship in heaven.

The increased prominence of Philippi in the time of Paul was due, however, not only to its advantages as a Roman colony, but still further to its geographical position. Through it ran the great Roman road, the *Via Egnatia,* from Dyrrhachium on the Adriatic Sea to Neapolis on the Aegean Sea, and eastward to the Hellespont. Its strategic military position had been recognized by Brutus and Cassius, but in the century which followed their defeat its importance as a commercial center rapidly advanced. Along the great Roman thoroughfare surged currents of life uniting the interests of the Far East with those of Roman Europe, and bringing to Philippi representatives of all races and of all religions.

It is not strange that Luke designated Philippi as "a city of Macedonia, the first of the district." As to the exact meaning of the latter phrase opinions differ. Some interpret it as designating Philippi as the first city a traveler would meet when entering Macedonia from the east. Less likely are the conjectures that it designated Philippi as the capital of the province, or the largest city of the province, for Thessalonica was the capital and Amphipolis, thirty-three miles to the southwest, surpassed Philippi in size; but because of its privileges as a Roman colony, and because of its strategic military and commercial position, Philippi properly might have been regarded as the most important city of that part of Macedonia.

In later centuries its importance gradually declined. Even the village of Filibejik, which until recent years preserved the name of Philippi, has now disappeared. Remains of the city, however, are abundant. Among these ruins are those of the great theater which faced toward Mt. Pangaeus, and those of the temple to the Roman god Silvanus, who was revered as the guardian of the emperor. The city has ceased to exist, but it is possibly glory enough for Philippi that it was the first city of Europe in which was established the church of Christ.

The Church at Philippi

The story of the founding of the church at Philippi, as related by Luke in the sixteenth chapter of The Acts, is fascinating and dramatic. Paul was on his second missionary journey. The first of these journeys had taken him from Antioch in Syria to the island of Cyprus, thence northward to what is now known as Asia Minor. There he established churches in Pisidian Antioch, in Iconium, in Lystra, and in Derbe. After the council at Jerusalem, about the year A.D. 50, he again started from Antioch, taking with him Silas as his companion. He revisited the churches at Derbe and Lystra and at the latter place was joined by Timothy, a young convert who became one of his closest friends and most valued helpers.

Still journeying westward, he apparently was planning to follow the Roman highways to Ephesus, the capital city of proconsular Asia. However, it was made plain to him by the Holy Spirit that he was not to preach in Asia at that time, and he therefore started northward to enter Bithynia. Again the "Spirit of Jesus" led him to alter his plan and, turning westward, he soon found himself at Troas, a seaport on the Aegean. Here the will of God became more clear. In a night vision he saw "a man of Macedonia standing, beseeching him, and saying, Come over into Macedonia, and help us." Luke adds, "And when he had seen the vision, straightway we sought to go forth into Macedonia, concluding that God had called us to preach the gospel unto them."

It is supposed that at this time Luke himself joined the company, for the change in the narrative from the third person to the first person, as shown by the pronouns "we" and "us," is a modest indication that the writer was an eyewitness of the events which he next relates. Indeed, there are those who suppose that Luke himself was a Macedonian, and that his meeting with Paul in Troas occasioned the dream by which the apostle was divinely guided to cross from Asia to Europe as a messenger of Christ.

Confident that they were following the leading of the Lord, Paul and his company set sail from Troas and after a short and prosperous voyage they landed at Neapolis. Without delay they pressed along the Egnatian Way some ten miles inland, crossing over the high mountain pass of Symbolum down onto the fertile plains which had been made famous by the victory of Octavian and Antony, and on into the colonial city of Philippi.

Usually Paul began his missionary work among the Jews. This was so at Antioch, at Lystra, at Thessalonica, and at Corinth. Evidently in Philippi there were few Jews to be found. No mention is made of a synagogue. However, on the Sabbath Day, Paul and his comrades went outside the city gates to a "place of prayer" on the banks of the river Gangites, where they found a number of women who had met to worship. Among them was one known as Lydia, possibly because she came from Thyatira, a city of Lydia in Asia Minor. She as described as "a seller of purple," that is, of purple dyes or of woolen fabrics dyed with the purple for which her native place was famous. She is further described as "one that worshipped God," by which is meant quite probably that she was a proselyte to Judaism. This woman gladly accepted the gospel message as delivered by Paul and was baptized, and thus became the first Christian convert on the continent of Europe. She showed her sincerity and devotion by leading to Christ her whole "household," by which is meant not only her family but her servants and dependents, and still further by constraining the company of missionaries to accept her hospitality during their stay in Philippi.

Lydia evidently was a woman of wealth and social standing and influence. Possibly to her assistance may be traced in some measure the immediate success of Paul's work and the further fact that the church which he founded in Philippi later showed its sympathetic interest by sending relief to the apostle and providing frequently for his needs. In any event, Lydia is a type of those God-fearing persons in every land who are in need of Christ and are yearning for the peace and light and life which Christ alone can give. Furthermore, she stands in the front rank of that great army of women who, through all the centuries, have furthered the preaching of the gospel by their hospitality, their sympathy, and their gifts.

Paul continued to attend "the place of prayer" and to preach freely until an incident occurred which brought upon him a tragic experience and gave a sudden ending to his stay in Philippi.

There was in the city a girl, apparently a slave, who was reputed to possess "a spirit of divination." Her soothsaying and ravings were enriching her masters through the fees they demanded of those who came to consult her. Day after day she followed Paul and Silas with the cry: "These men are servants of the Most High God, who proclaim unto you the way of salvation." Paul did not wish testimony from such a questionable source. Moreover, he desired to set the poor girl free, not only from her masters but from the spirit by which she was tormented. Thus, as the story runs, "Paul, being sore troubled, turned and said to the spirit, I charge thee in the name of Jesus Christ to come out of her. And it came out that very hour."

This poor girl, rather than Lydia, is the type of womanhood found in Christless lands. There, commonly, women are the slaves or toys or tools of men. Their degradation and nameless agonies constitute the real Macedonian cry, which the church should heed and in obedience to which it should hasten to bring relief. The deepest distress of these sufferers is due, however, not merely to social and physical conditions. Their supreme need is to be delivered from the evil spirits which control their hearts. They are awaiting messengers who, like Paul, can effect release in the omnipotent name of Christ.

The healing of the slave girl in Philippi aroused the fierce anger of her masters. There are men today willing to acquire wealth and power, not only by cruel forms of child labor but by the degrading of womanhood and the exploiting of weakness, who resent as an impertinent intrusion every attempt to deliver their helpless victims. Thus these men of old regarded the action of Paul. "When her masters saw that the hope of their gain was gone, they laid hold on Paul and Silas, and dragged them into the marketplace before the rulers." They assumed the air not only of injured innocence but of ardent patriotism as they declared that they had no selfish interest at stake but were concerned for the public good. Even so men at the present time grow eloquent on the subject of imperiled liberties when laws are enacted which check their ill-gotten gains.

The slave girl's masters dragged Paul and Silas to the magistrates with the charge: "These men, being Jews, do exceedingly trouble our city, and set forth customs which it is not lawful for us to receive, or to observe, being Romans." It was a clever appeal to popular prejudice, for the people prided themselves upon their Roman citizenship and would be enraged at Jews who were accused of endangering or disrespecting their rights. A gathering mob threatened violence and the magistrates, or "praetors," in an apparent frenzy of rage, ordered their attendants, or "lictors," to scourge Paul and his companion, overlooking the possibility of their being Roman citizens. Cruelly beaten, bleeding, and helpless, the evangelists were cast into the public prison. They were placed in the innermost ward and their feet made fast in the stocks. However, at midnight the other prisoners heard them praying and singing praises to God.

Suddenly the prison was shaken by an earthquake. All doors were opened and all bonds loosed. The jailer, startled out of his sleep, was about to kill himself, thinking that the prisoners had escaped and that his life would be held forfeit. Paul, however, "cried with a loud voice, saying, Do thyself no harm: for we are all here."

Calling for a light, and falling down before Paul and Silas, the jailer uttered his pitiful cry, "Sirs, what must I do to be saved?" It is a cry which those who will listen may hear in every land, a cry addressed to all the followers of Christ, a cry expressing the supreme need of every human soul. Paul and Silas gave the memorable reply, "Believe on the Lord Jesus, and thou shalt be saved, thou and thy house." The jailer's eager acceptance of the teaching of the apostles, his kindly care for their wounds, his immediate confession of his faith, his securing of the same confession from the members of his household, all witness to the clear understanding and sincere acceptance of the salvation offered in the name of Christ.

This jailer stands in striking contrast to the two other converts who are so prominent in the story, Lydia and the slave girl. The former of these held a respected social position, and was engaged in a profitable trade. The latter was a mere piece of property, used by her masters to defraud ignorant and credulous victims. The jailer held a minor and despised office under the local government. One of these three converts was a Jewess or a proselyte to Judaism from Asia; one was a Greek; one, a Roman. All three alike accepted the Christian message, and illustrate its adaptation to all classes and races and conditions of men. They were the first fruits of the gospel on the continent of Europe, and their experiences formed a prophecy of what this gospel was to achieve in the emancipation of slaves, in the ennobling of human life, and in the establishment of the Christian home.

In the morning the magistrates, no doubt alarmed by the report of what had occurred, gave orders that Paul and Silas should be released, but Paul sent back word demanding a public vindication and terrified the rulers by the announcement that he was a Roman citizen. Possibly Paul had made the same claim when he was scourged, but in the confusion and excitement his claim had been unheeded or even unheard. The magistrates had been guilty of a serious offense against the laws of Rome. They had beaten and imprisoned a citizen who was uncondemned. Now they hastened to the prison, showing Paul and his companion all deference and respect, and pleaded with them to leave the city. This Paul consented to do. His victory had been complete. He had made the civil authorities understand that in showing violence to citizens for their Christian faith they might be offending against the laws of the state and the laws of God.

After visiting the house of Lydia and encouraging the Christian brethren who were meeting there, Paul departed from Philippi. He left in the city a flourishing Christian church, which through all the following years held a chief place in his heart. The friends he had made in Philippi followed his movements with deepest interest and affection. Again and again they sent gifts to supply his needs. More than once during the following years the apostle returned to visit them.

The church at Philippi, however, was one which continually suffered from poverty and persecution. Its last mention in history is in connection with a visit from the Christian martyr Ignatius, when he was on his way to suffer death in Rome. Thus in the very dawn of the Christian era the church at Philippi disappeared from sight; yet to it belongs an immortality of fame and glory because of this single letter addressed to it by the apostle Paul.

The Occasion of the Letter

The Epistle of Paul to the Philippians was occasioned by a gift sent to the apostle by the Philippian church. This remembrance was brought by the hand of Epaphroditus, who had requested the privilege not only of being a messenger of the church but also of remaining with Paul to serve and comfort him during the days of his imprisonment. However, Epaphroditus had been taken seriously ill. For a time Paul despaired of his life. Word of his illness had reached the Philippians and they shared in the keen anxiety of the apostle. On his recovery Epaphroditus, as well as Paul, desired to relieve the friends in Philippi of their fears. Therefore, Paul sent Epaphroditus back home and took the opportunity of dispatching with him this letter. It was intended to express to the Philippians his thanks for their gift. Paul naturally gave his friends information as to his own situation and experiences, and offered them such advice as seemed necessary in view of the report brought by Epaphroditus as to the condition of the church. The main purpose of the letter, however, was to convey to the Philippians the grateful recognition of their gift, while the immediate occasion was the return of Epaphroditus to Philippi.

Paul was at the time a prisoner. Was the scene of this imprisonment Caesarea or Ephesus or Corinth or Rome? The traditional view fixes upon Rome. Among the facts supporting this view are the mention of the "prætorian guard," the reference to "Cæsar's household," and the description of Paul's circumstances, which seem to correspond with those of his imprisonment as depicted by Luke in The Acts. For example, there was near him a large and active church. He was enjoying the fellowship of many friends, old and new, who had free access to him, and his trial, with its decisive issue, was just at hand. All this indicates that Rome was the scene of his imprisonment.

However, there are many students who argue strenuously, if not convincingly, for Caesarea, and others, even more recently, for Ephesus. It is true that Paul was imprisoned for two years at Caesarea, and he may have been imprisoned at Ephesus, although there is no statement in the New Testament to substantiate that theory. It is also true that the word πραιτώριον, translated "prætorian guard," might designate the residence of a provincial governor in Caesarea, or the soldiers of the Praetorian Guard stationed at Ephesus. However, the specific statements that "the saints . . . of Cæsar's household" united with Paul in his greetings to the Philippians, and more particularly the fact that his imprisonment was soon to end, and possibly by a sentence of death, point rather definitely to Rome as the place of captivity.

Other theories, though ardently advocated, seem based on conjectures and suppositions, while the generally accepted view rests upon some unquestioned certainties. Paul undoubtedly was imprisoned at least once in Rome. There was also in Rome a Praetorian Guard, and surely members of Caesar's household were there. Furthermore, when Paul reached the city as a prisoner, as definitely recorded by Luke, there existed a church of exactly the character plainly depicted by the apostle in his letter to the Philippians.

Therefore, it would seem that some ten or eleven years had passed since the founding of the church. When Paul left Philippi he continued his missionary journey southward to Athens and Corinth and then eastward to Caesarea and Jerusalem and Antioch. On his succeeding journey he remained for nearly three years in Ephesus and then passed through Macedonia on his way to Greece. In all probability he stopped for some time at Philippi as he journeyed, and there wrote his second letter to the Corinthians. After spending three months in Greece he returned to Macedonia and spent the Passover with his Philippian friends. Turning eastward with the collection he had secured for the needy Christians in Jerusalem, his journey ended in the sacred city. There, however, he was arrested and taken thence for safe-keeping to Caesarea. After a long delay, and despairing of justice, he made his appeal to Caesar and ultimately was dispatched to Rome. He had been longing for an opportunity to preach the gospel in the Imperial City and to strengthen the church already established there. This for years had been his dream. However, he had not imagined that he would be brought to his goal as a prisoner in chains. Nevertheless, his hopes were not wholly frustrated. He did find opportunities for preaching the "good news." The Christians in Rome welcomed him gladly and they witnessed for Christ the more boldly because of his presence among them. Some, however, who preached the gospel were animated by a spirit of envy and enmity toward Paul, and preached with the aim of causing faction. They probably were not the extreme Judaizers whom Paul rebuked in other letters, but still they were adding Jewish legal elements to the pure gospel of grace which the apostle proclaimed.

Then, too, Paul was under the deepening shadow of impending death. However, there was much to cheer him. He was allowed a very considerable degree of liberty. About him was a circle of trusted companions. Friends arrived from distant lands with news from the churches he had founded. Prominent among the latter was Epaphroditus, of Philippi, who brought the precious gift, the acknowledgment of which was the occasion or purpose of this letter.

There were, however, other epistles which were written at about this same time. Ephesians, Colossians, and Philemon are also known as "letters of Paul's imprisonment." In what order of time were these epistles composed? By common consent Philippians stands by itself, while the other three, because of their distinct character and purpose and content, form a separate group and appear to have been composed at a different period of time.

Was Philippians written before or after these companion epistles? Those who place Philippians first among these four letters argue chiefly from its likeness to Romans and First and Second Corinthians and Galatians, which were written some five years before Paul's imprisonment. This argument is precarious and is supported by no positive evidence.

On the other hand, there is no one fact which makes it absolutely necessary to place Philippians last among these letters. In either case it is evident that some considerable time had elapsed since Paul reached the city of Rome. News of his imprisonment had been carried to the Philippians. From this church Epaphroditus had been sent to bring Paul relief. This messenger, after his long journey, had suffered a lingering and desperate illness. Word of his sickness had been carried to Philippi, and news of the anxiety felt by his friends had been brought back to Rome. Also, Epaphroditus had recovered and was so far restored to health that he was ready for his arduous homeward journey.

Furthermore, it appears that Luke and Aristarchus, who accompanied Paul to Rome and were with him when he wrote to the Colossians, were not sharing his imprisonment when the letter to the Philippians was composed, for in this letter he expressed his loneliness, stating, too, that with the exception of Timothy the Christians about him "all seek their own, not the things of Jesus Christ."

Then again the picture given of the church in Rome indicates that the apostle had been present in the city for some time. The quickening of life and the renewal of activity caused by the influence of Paul indicate, not a sudden process, but a substantial progress which for its accomplishment must have required a considerable period of time. So, too, wide circles in the city, outside the church, have been affected, and this could not have resulted early in Paul's imprisonment. Furthermore, Paul is certain that the issue of his trial is near at hand.

When, therefore, it is remembered that this entire imprisonment occupied probably not more than two years, it is evident that the epistle could not have been written very far from the end of that period, whether it was composed before or after the other letters of this imprisonment. However, this is not a question of great importance. Neither view affects the interpretation of any vital statement of doctrine, nor of its application to practical life; nor does the belief that it was written later in his imprisonment carry with it the theory that at this time the nature of Paul's confinement had changed and was more harsh and rigorous than at first. There is no sufficient ground furnished by the epistle to substantiate this conjecture.

It may be concluded, therefore, that the Epistle to the Philippians was written by Paul when a prisoner in Rome about the year A.D. 63. He was in close communication with the Christians of the city. He was receiving and dispatching messengers and letters from and to distant churches. Four of these epistles have come down to us. In this particular letter the apostle expresses his gratitude and offers his affectionate counsel on the occasion of receiving a gift from that church which was the first he founded in Europe and which during all the passing years was nearest to his heart.

THE CHARACTER OF THE LETTER

The story of the founding of the church at Philippi and the circumstances under which this letter was written are brought to mind continually throughout the whole course of the epistle. It is recalled that Philippi was a Roman colony; so the readers are urged to exercise their citizenship in a manner worthy of the gospel (ch. 1:27); and, further, to remember that their true citizenship is in heaven (ch. 3:20). In the establishment of the church, women had a chief place; so in the letter women are mentioned as occupying a position of prominence among the Christian believers. Furthermore, when Paul first visited Philippi Lydia aided the apostle by her gracious hospitality; so the letter is written to thank the Philippians for their assistance in furthering the gospel by their generous gift sent to relieve the apostle's needs. When at Philippi Paul had been scourged and imprisoned, but he sang songs in the night until the prison was shaken; so after the lapse of years Paul is now a prisoner in Rome, yet he writes this letter which is a veritable paean of praise. The first converts at Philippi demonstrated the transforming power of faith, and here is an epistle which is at once a monument to the saving influence of the gospel and a witness to the sustaining grace of the living Christ. The composition is furthermore a letter of love. It has been called the most personal of all Paul's epistles. This is true if possibly Philemon and Second Corinthians are excepted. However, a letter may be intensely personal and yet be not at all affectionate; unfortunately such letters are not unfamiliar. Here, however, is a composition which from first to last overflows with expressions of personal devotion. There is nothing studied or conventional in its style. Everything is spontaneous and informal. A friend is pouring out his heart to those whom he loves. No set form or rigid order of thought is followed. The apostle is attempting to teach no specific doctrines. Nor is he defending Christian truth against its foes. This is a letter of thanksgiving for sympathy which has been generously expressed. It states artlessly items of personal news and abounds in outbursts of true affection.

Paul is thankful for every remembrance of his Philippian friends. (Ch. 1:3.) He praises them as beloved brethren and prays that their love "may abound yet more and more in knowledge and all discernment" (v. 9). He rejoices in the privilege of being "offered upon the sacrifice and service of [their] . . . faith" (ch. 2:17). He describes his friends as "beloved and longed for," as his "joy and crown."

Yet his love does not blind him to a defect in the Philippians which has been reported. They had some tendency to show envy and faction and lack of harmony. They were in some danger from influences which might lead to formalism or to lawlessness. Nevertheless, whatever the epistle may contain in the form of exhortations to harmony and self-forgetful service, or of warnings against Judaistic teaching and wrong conduct, these are quite incidental and due to Paul's solicitude for the welfare of his friends, and are not to be regarded as the causes or the characteristic features of the letter.

Paul is writing as one who is sure of his place in the hearts of his readers, and he wishes them to be sure of the place they hold in his. This deep affection may be traced to the open-heartedness of those Macedonian Christians, and to their natural frankness and simplicity and genuine affection. They had not been weaned away from the apostle by false teachers, as had the Christians in Galatia. Furthermore, they had shown their loyalty previously by deeds of love, sending to the apostle repeated remembrances; and when he had appealed to them in behalf of the needy Christians in Jerusalem, he had been astonished at the liberality and self-sacrifice of their response. It is not strange that the Christians in Philippi held a deeper place in his affection than the members of any other church and that in recognizing their kindness he gives such artless expressions of his love.

This is, moreover, a letter of joy. As a famous commentator has said, *"Summa epistolae, gaudeo gaudete"*— "The sum of the epistle is 'I rejoice; rejoice ye.'" Paul's circumstancs were not such as to awaken this emotion. In fact one of the main messages of the epistle is the truth that joy need not be conditioned upon outward circumstances. There was much in Paul's surroundings to produce gloom and depression. Bonds and imprisonment had interrupted his untiring journeys and his far-reaching plans. He was comparatively alone and without the comfort of close friends and the inspiration of great audiences. An active section of the Roman church was attempting to distress him by its distorted message. The future was dark with uncertainty, and a martyr's death might at any time overtake him. However, throughout the whole letter, breaking through the overhanging clouds, rises the clarion note of the undaunted apostle, "Rejoice . . . again I will say, Rejoice." Some twenty times in the short space of these four chapters we read such words as "joy," "rejoice," "thanksgiving," "content," and "peace."

However, this is a letter of faith. The love is for those who are "in Christ Jesus." The joy is the joy of the Lord. The whole message is from one who found in Christ the sum and substance of his life. To preach the gospel of Christ was Paul's consuming passion and his unfailing occupation. His chief desire for his friends was that they might "be of the same mind in the Lord." To attain to the moral likeness and perfection of Christ was his constant effort. That he could do all things in the power of Christ was his unfailing comfort and his abiding hope. Surely here was one who could say with all sincerity, "To me to live is Christ."

It is this fact which gives to the epistle its real character. Here is a letter abounding in love and joy because the writer is united to Christ by a living faith. He writes out of his imprisonment to his distant friends to tell them of his affection and his hopes; and all that concerns him is so vitally related to his Lord that the letter can be regarded as the epistle which, more than any other, sets forth Paul's experimental knowledge of Christ. It inspires the reader to seek a closer fellowship with that living Christ who ever imparts love and joy and makes his followers fruitful in his service.

THE CONTENTS OF THE LETTER

An epistle so personal and informal was not composed according to any fixed plan. Therefore it cannot be submitted to strict logical analysis. However, it is not at all difficult to trace its general and quite natural order of thought.

As was his custom, Paul opens the letter with a salutation, a giving of thanks, and a prayer. These, however, are unusually prolonged, possibly because of the intensity of emotion by which the writer was stirred. In the salutation, Paul unites with his own the name of his beloved companion, Timothy, and, as in no other letter, he specifies the "bishops" and "deacons" of the church as the special recipients of his greeting. (Ch. 1:1-2.)

His thanksgiving is based upon his personal relations to the readers, for whom he states his tender affection. He expresses gratitude for their fellowship in the work of the gospel, and for the confident assurance that God will continue in them his good work until the day of Christ's return. (Vs. 3-8.)

In his prayer for them Paul makes request that their love may issue in higher spiritual knowledge, so that they may be able to discriminate wisely and choose the things that are best; so that they may be sincere and free from offense, "being filled with the fruits of righteousness." (Vs. 9-11.)

Paul then begins the main portion of his letter by an account of his personal situation and experiences in Rome. Everything is turning out well for the advance of the gospel and Paul is filled with joy. It is true that he suffers as a prisoner, but none the less he rejoices for the opportunities thus afforded for making known the "good tidings." He is chained to one soldier after another, but this gives an opportunity for personal conversations. Other soldiers have paused to listen and the message has been spread throughout the whole Praetorian Guard. (Vs. 12-13.)

Throughout the whole city Christian believers have been made more bold in their witness for Christ because of the presence of Paul. It is true that some are animated by motives of envy and ill will toward the apostle, even as others are motivated by love. In either case Paul rejoices, for Christ is being preached, whether by enemies or by friends. (Vs. 15-18.)

The result of his impending trial is uncertain. It may issue in his discharge or his death, and it is difficult for him to decide which he should prefer. He has the confident hope that Christ will be magnified in him whether by life or by death. For him life is summed up in the service of Christ, and death will bring him into an even more glorious fellowship with Christ. Therefore death is the more attractive prospect. However, if to live means that more fruit will result from his labors, then he may well hope to live. Indeed, he has an instinctive belief that he is to live because the churches are so greatly in need of his guidance and help. (Vs. 19-26.)

He therefore exhorts his readers to live in a manner worthy of the gospel of Christ, manifesting unity in effort and service and steadfastness in the face of persecution, imitating Paul, their fellow soldier, who in the same conflict has stood firm in the faith. (Vs. 27-30.)

Paul further appeals to the Philippians to make his joy full by manifesting that unity which can be produced only by "lowliness of mind." (Ch. 2:1-4.) Of such true humility and self-forgetful service the supreme example is Christ. His voluntary exchange of the form of God for the form of a servant and his obedience even unto shame and death are an inspiration to lowliness, while his supreme exaltation is an encouragement to patient endurance, as it shows God's certain reward of humility and self-sacrifice. (Vs. 5-11.)

In view of this example Paul further exhorts his readers to obedience, to serious spiritual effort, to mutual forbearance, and to conduct that is becoming to children of God, that in the darkness of the present they may appear as "lights in the world," and that he who has labored for their salvation may receive his due recompense when Christ returns. Paul is ready even now to pour out his life as a libation to the sacrifice and service of their faith. (Vs. 12-18.)

Paul now returns to matters of a more personal character. He mentions his plans for the future as they concern two of his friends, Timothy and Epaphroditus. He intends to send the former to Philippi as soon as he learns the issue of his impending trial. As to this trial he is hopeful of a favorable outcome, in which case he will himself come shortly to visit the church he so loves. (Vs. 19-24.)

As to Epaphroditus, he is dispatching him with this letter. Gladly would he have retained in Rome this faithful messenger who had brought the welcome remembrance from Philippi, but Epaphroditus has been seriously ill, and, though now recovered, is homesick for his friends in distant Macedonia. He longs to return, and thus Paul takes the occasion of sending this epistle, and of cordially commending Epaphroditus for his courage and his self-sacrificing service. (Vs. 25-30.)

Here Paul seems about to bring the letter to a close, but he turns rather abruptly to warn his readers against two classes who might exert an evil influence by their teachings or their example. The first are those who are characterized by formalism; the second, those characterized by lawlessness. In contrast with both, the apostle ventures to suggest himself as an example. Against the first class he delivers an impassioned invective. They were the legalists who ever were insisting upon introducing among Christians the rites of the Jews. He regards them as worshiping in the flesh and not in the Spirit of God. As to fleshly privileges, Paul claims all that these Judaizers could boast, but he has renounced all these that he may gain Christ in their stead. He wishes to know Christ more perfectly in all his transforming power with its final issue in a glorious resurrection. (Ch. 3:1-11.)

Paul does not regard himself as having yet attained to all the blessedness of the Christian calling, but, like a runner in the race, he is forgetting the things behind and pressing forward toward the goal for the prize he is yet to receive. He urges all who claim spiritual maturity to follow in his steps. (Vs. 12-16.)

There is, however, another class, even among Christians, who go to the other extreme. They are regarded as enemies of the cross of Christ, not because of false teaching, but because of their lawless and impure living. They "mind earthly things." True Christians, however, regard heaven as the place of their citizenship and look for the coming of the Savior, who will transform their bodies as well as their spirits into his own glorious likeness. (Vs. 17-21.)

Here the thread of the letter is again resumed and Paul exhorts his readers to steadfastness and unity. This exhortation is specially addressed to two women, Euodia and Syntyche. Another friend of the apostle is urged to effect, if possible, a reconciliation between these who had formerly labored with the apostle and belonged to that band of faithful workers "whose names are in the book of life." (Ch. 4:1-3.) Then all the church is exhorted to joyfulness and forbearance and to trust in God, whose peace will stand sentinel over their hearts and minds. (Vs. 4-7.)

Paul furthermore summons the Philippians to high thought and to noble endeavor, again venturing to give himself as an example and assuring them of the gracious presence of the God of peace. (Vs. 8-9.)

At last, in the very closing paragraphs of this informal epistle, the apostle discloses the chief practical purpose of the letter, which is to voice his gratitude to his friends in Philippi for their gracious gift delivered by the hand of Epaphroditus. This gratitude is phrased with delicate and considerate courtesy. He recognizes that the good will of the Philippians toward him had never failed, and that it had not taken practical form earlier in his imprisonment only for lack of opportunity.

He intimates his own independence of material conditions, because he had learned the secret of contentment as he relied upon the power of Christ. However, he gratefully acknowledges their exceptional kindness to him on this as on previous occasions. He values their remembrance not only for its own worth but for the spirit in which it is given. He knows that it is a sacrifice "well-pleasing to God" and that in return God will supply all their need "according to his riches in glory in Christ Jesus." This message of gratitude to Paul's friends ends with a doxology of praise to God. (Vs. 10-20.) The letter closes with salutations, and with the benediction, "The grace of the Lord Jesus Christ be with your spirit." (Vs. 21-23.)

THE OUTLINE

I
THE PREFACE
Phil. 1:1-11

A. THE SALUTATION   Ch. 1:1-2

1 Paul and Timothy, servants of Christ Jesus, to all the saints in Christ Jesus that are at Philippi, with the bishops and deacons: 2 Grace to you and peace from God our Father and the Lord Jesus Christ.

The name of Paul, which stands at the head of this epistle, gives to the whole letter its deepest interest, its true significance, its abiding worth.   That Paul was its author there can be no reasonable doubt.   It may have been written by his own hand.   Probably it was dictated to a scribe. In either event it came out of Paul's very heart.   It reflects the circumstances and reveals the character of the great apostle with a clearness which it would be difficult to question or mistake.

True it is, however, that the Paul revealed here seems to differ in some respects from the Paul who wrote the epistles to the Romans, to the Corinthians, and to the Galatians.   This difference is due, however, to a change in conditions and a difference in purpose.   Paul is now a prisoner.   He is so advanced in years or so worn by his labors that he describes himself in a companion epistle as "Paul the aged."   Furthermore, he is writing, not to establish doctrines or to correct errors in belief or practice, but to express his gratitude and affection to certain of his friends.

He is in Rome.   After his three long missionary journeys he has been arrested in Jerusalem and then imprisoned at Caesarea.   Learning of a plot against his life and despairing of justice from the provincial governor, he has made his "appeal unto Cæsar," and finally has been brought to the Imperial City. While awaiting trial he has been allowed a considerable degree of freedom and permitted to communicate freely with his friends. From distant Philippi, at the hand of Epaphroditus, he has received a rich gift. To acknowledge this remembrance he is writing this letter. Naturally it expresses a different side of his character from that revealed in the earlier epistles. There he is the acute logician, the profound theologian, the stern defender of the faith. Here he appears as the affectionate friend, the man of tender heart, of human sympathies, of deep emotions, of tears, and of joy.

But it is the same great apostle. Here he is writing a brief fugitive note to an obscure Christian church, but his message is so phrased as to add to his own imperishable fame and to be worthy of its place among his immortal epistles, which have immeasurably enriched the literature of the world. He shows that it is possible to perform insignificant duties with such a spirit as to rejoice the hearts of friends and to gild the humblest deeds with a light which never fades.

This epistle is distinctly Paul's own. It is written in the first person singular. However, in the salutation, Paul unites with his own name that of Timothy. This beloved comrade, by his presence and help, is cheering Paul in his imprisonment. Paul had a genius for friendship and Timothy seems to have held the first place in his affection. Their acquaintance dated from the time when Paul, on his first missionary journey, had visited Lystra, where Timothy lived. The father of Timothy was a Greek and it is probable that Timothy enjoyed the culture which this term implies. What is more certain and more important, he was brought up under strong religious influences; his mother, Eunice, like his grandmother, Lois, was a devout Jewess, and from his earliest years Timothy was instructed carefully in the Holy Scriptures.

It was during the impressionable days of Timothy's boyhood that Paul made his memorable visit to Lystra, where the populace first wished to worship the apostle and later sought to take his life. Timothy seems to have listened with eagerness to the "good news" preached by Paul. He saw him heal a helpless cripple, heard him appeal to the listening crowds, looked on in horror when the apostle was stoned and left as dead, and gazed in wonder when Paul arose and reentered the city. The next day the apostle had started on his journey, but in the company of Christian converts whom he had left behind in Lystra were Eunice and her son Timothy.

On his second missionary journey, Paul had revisited Lystra and while there had chosen Timothy as his companion in travel. This choice was determined in part by the high esteem in which the young disciple was held by the Christians both of Lystra and of Iconium, and further by certain prophetic utterances which intimated the fitness of Timothy for his task. Timothy must have revealed also certain traits of character which appealed to Paul and won his confidence and love. Apparently he was a man of sensitive and affectionate disposition, somewhat timid and not physically robust, but possessing a personality of peculiar beauty and depth and charm. He became the friend of Paul's bosom. Together they journeyed westward, crossed the Aegean, and at Philippi founded the first church in Europe. Henceforth Timothy accompanied Paul on all his journeys or accepted from him difficult and delicate missions to distant chuches. The very last of all his letters was written by Paul to Timothy, summoning him to solace his last hours before the aged apostle was led forth to a martyr's death.

It is natural, then, that the name of this friend, who at the time was with Paul in Rome, should be mentioned as the apostle begins his letter to the Philippians. It is even more natural in view of the fact that at this particular time of Paul's imprisonment Timothy was the only friend who could be relied upon for sympathy and aid. It is even possible that Timothy was acting as Paul's secretary and writing this letter as it was dictated by the apostle.

Then again, Timothy was well-known to the Philippians whom Paul was addressing. He had been with them often and was soon to visit them again. They would be pleased by this mention of his name; and as for Timothy, it must have thrilled his heart that his distinguished friend, in such a connection, should have associated their two names. Whatever the conscious motive, it was a touch of delicate courtesy on the part of the greathearted apostle. It also is an illustration of the power true friendship has to glorify and to inspire.

Paul introduces both Timothy and himself as "servants of Christ Jesus." More usually he assumed the title of "apostle." The latter would be quite natural when writing a letter in which it was necessary to insist upon his authority, to defend some doctrine, or to enforce some command. Here, however, such a word would be out of place, for all the letter is friendly, personal, and informal. The term "servants," or, literally, "bondservants," is one of true humility, yet when united with the name of "Christ Jesus" it is a word of real dignity. It denotes dependence, obedience, acknowledged ownership. However, it has no implication of servility or of compulsory service. It indicates intense devotion and that willing obedience which is perfect freedom. Indeed, the term had become familiar from Old Testament usage as one of high honor. It was applied to the prophets and messengers of Jehovah. They were "servants" of the Most High. Thus Paul here identifies himself and Timothy with the cause of Christ as men who belong wholly to the Lord and are acting in his name.

Even the order of the two words, "Christ Jesus," instead of "Jesus Christ" is characteristic of Paul. He usually thinks, not of the man "Jesus" who proved to be the "Christ," but of the exalted "Christ" who was once the man "Jesus." It is the divine, the omnipotent, the reigning Christ who is ever in the mind of the apostle. Some scholars question this distinction; indeed it is made uncertain by the reading found in many Greek manuscripts; but it is a view worthy of most careful thought.

Paul designates himself and Timothy as "servants"; he describes his readers as "saints." There is undoubted humility in such a contrast, when he addresses his epistle "to all the saints in Christ Jesus that are at Philippi." "Saints" was the common term applied in the time of Paul to all Christians. It was the equivalent of "believers" or "brethren." It indicated all the members of the Christian church. However, its deep significance and implication must not be forgotten. Its root idea is that of separation, and particularly of consecration. It describes those who are set aside to a sacred use, those who are consecrated to God. Furthermore, it implies that those so consecrated should be "holy ones" in their character and life.

It was a term applied frequently to Israel as the chosen people of God, set apart from the nations for his service. Quite naturally it was adopted by Christians as the proper designation of the church, which was "an elect race, a royal priesthood, a holy nation," called out from both Jews and Gentiles as the elect people of God. It is an ideal term, indicating not moral perfection, but such a relation to God as makes purity of heart and conduct an obligation for all to whom the term is applied. Yet it implies, not only a duty, but a glorious privilege. It is an inspiration to Christian believers to know that they are "saints." They are encouraged to become in actual experience what they already are in the mind and purpose of God.

The Jews might claim the term as belonging to them; therefore Paul adds the words, "In Christ Jesus." This last phrase is the most significant and characteristic of any that appears in his writings. It has been regarded rightfully as the sum of his religion. It occurs eight times in this epistle. In his letters as a whole he uses "in Christ" thirty-seven times, "in Christ Jesus" forty-one times, "in the Lord" forty-three times. The phrases seem to be original with Paul. By them he means to describe the closest union which can be conceived between the believer and his living Lord. For the true Christian, all plans and purposes, all activities, all hopes are in Christ. "In Christ" he is "a new creature." For him "to live is Christ."

To those who are consecrated to the service of God, to those who are "in Christ Jesus," it matters little where they may reside. Those whom Paul addressed lived "at Philippi." This city is illustrious, not so much for its historic association with the names of Brutus and Cassius, Octavian and Antony, but because of the "saints" who once resided there, and because of its connection with the life of Paul. At least three times he visited the city. The description of his first visit, which resulted in the founding of the church, is related in The Acts and is full and vivid. When, on his third missionary journey, he hastened on from Troas to meet Titus, he probably tarried in Philippi and wrote his Second Epistle to the Corinthians. Again on his return from Greece he remained in Philippi to observe the Feast of the Passover. Yet wherever he journeyed his friends in Philippi followed him with loving interest, and now in writing to express his appreciation and love, he addresses them as "saints."

Too commonly we associate that term with the holy dead. The apostle uses it of residents in the thronging centers of Corinth, of Colossae, or of Rome. It was not in a celestial city that these "saints" at Philippi were dwelling, but in a Roman military town, with its vices and cruelties, its superstitions and degradation, its markets and its temples, its angry mob, its proud magistrates, and its dark dungeons. One of these "saints" was a woman merchant, one a slave girl, one the keeper of a jail. Yet they all were "in Christ Jesus." All were witnesses to the power of the living Lord. Together they formed a Christian church.

In addressing this church Paul specifies "the bishops

and deacons." This is unique. The words occur in the salutation of no other epistle. Furthermore, it is, in order of time, the first mention in the New Testament of these church officers. Probably they are designated as the particular members of the church who had suggested and had forwarded the gift to the apostle. Possibly they are mentioned in courteous recognition of their position and standing among the Philippian Christians. This allusion to "bishops and deacons" has led to endless discussion and speculation. It opens the whole question of the Christian ministry and of the organization and government of the Christian church.

As to church government there are two extreme views. One holds that no organization is necessary and that there should be no ordained officers among the body of believers. The other insists that some particular form of organization is essential to the very existence of a church. The true view should be that a form of government is necessary, not to the being, but to the well-being of a church. Any form should be allowed which does not violate such great Scriptural principles as the universal priesthood of believers and the vital Headship of Christ. Probably no existing form is an exact reproduction of the organization of the primitive church. That original form appears to have been extremely simple. It became more complex as circumstances seemed to demand.

The "bishops" of the New Testament were identical with the "elders," or "presbyters." Their duty was that of "overseers." Some of them taught but all exercised spiritual rule or guidance and all were on a perfect equality as officers in the local churches. No one was regarded as holding a place of authority superior to others. From this one office with its different functions various offices have been developed. In some communions the "bishop" has been assigned oversight of a group of churches, while the "presbyter," or "priest," has been given the leadership of the individual congregation. In other communions the

"bishop," or "pastor," or "minister," is given the functions of preaching and of conducting public worship, and
is designated as a clergyman, while the "elders" are regarded as laymen and, in cooperation with the "pastor,"
act as the spiritual rulers of the local church.

The origin of the office of "deacon" may be traced to
the incident recorded in the sixth chapter of The Acts
when the "seven" were elected and ordained to assist the
apostles; they were to "serve tables" and exercise care of
those members of the church who were in need. Although
the nature of the office cannot be established beyond question, there does seem to be a distinction of function among
the ministers of the apostolic churches. Some had duties
to perform which were specifically spiritual; some were assigned to tasks more directly concerned with the temporal
affairs of the congregation. Such a distinction is wise and
is usually maintained in the practice of the modern church.

Whatever were the exact functions of the "elders" and
"deacons," they are mentioned after the "saints," which
may be an intimation that they were not regarded as of
superior importance. They were, as Christian "ministers"
ever should be, the servants, or leaders, or superintendents
of the congregation, never the masters or lords of the
Christian heritage.

In his salutation to the Philippian church Paul does not
use the word which expresses "greeting." The full formula, according to the custom of the day might have been
as follows: "Paul and Timothy send greeting to all the
saints at Philippi." Paul, however, transforms the conventional salutation into a Christian prayer: "Grace to you
and peace from God our Father and the Lord Jesus
Christ." He really plays upon the word used for greeting
(Greek, χαίρειν) and it becomes "grace" (Greek, χάρις),
denoting the unmerited favor of God and including in its
meaning all the boundless blessings secured for man by the
redeeming love of God. To this word, which is an ennobled form of the Greek salutation, Paul adds the char-

acteristic Hebrew greeting, "Peace be with you." This
again is immeasurably enriched by being related to God
and to Christ. It is that peace which can come only
through the "grace" of God. It is peace with God, peace
with men, peace in the inner recesses of one's being. In
describing the divine source from which Paul expects this
grace and peace to flow, Paul places "the Lord Jesus
Christ" on an equality with "God our Father." He thus
expresses the Christian conception of the loving Father-
hood of God and the divine nature of Christ. The latter is
unquestionably denoted by the term "Lord." It was familiar from its Old Testament usage as a designation of the
divine Being. It was employed in Paul's day to designate
the emperor, who claimed divine honor and worship.

Thus the phrase "Lord Jesus Christ" has a marvelous
wealth of meaning. "Jesus" was the human, personal
name of the Savior. "Christ" was his official title, as the
"Anointed One" who had been appointed and empowered
to accomplish salvation for mankind. "Lord" was the
title which denoted the true deity recognized by all who
accepted him as Master and worshiped him as the Son
of God.

This salutation which opens the epistle to the Philippians is familiar, almost conventional, in form, but its
meaning must not be dulled like the image on a well-worn
coin. It points the reader to the very heart of the letter,
in which Paul expresses his true affection for his friends
and also reveals his personal experience in the knowledge
of Jesus Christ as his loving Master, his living Lord.

B. THE THANKSGIVING   Ch. 1:3-8

*3 I thank my God upon all my remembrance of you,
4 always in every supplication of mine on behalf of you
all making my supplication with joy, 5 for your fellowship
in furtherance of the gospel from the first day until now;
6 being confident of this very thing, that he who began a
good work in you will perfect it until the day of Jesus*

Christ: 7 even as it is right for me to be thus minded on behalf of you all, because I have you in my heart, inasmuch as, both in my bonds and in the defence and confirmation of the gospel, ye all are partakers with me of grace. 8 For God is my witness, how I long after you all in the tender mercies of Christ Jesus.

Friendship has ever been regarded rightfully as a priceless gift, as indeed a chief factor in giving to life its breadth and beauty, its inspiration, and its joy. Even the most masterful and courageous of men have felt in their hearts a constant hunger for human sympathy and love. Such a man was Paul. Probably many strong and tender ties had been severed by his sudden conversion from Judaism to Christianity. His affections sought new channels and henceforth were poured out upon his fellow believers. Loneliness was ever one of his greatest trials, and companionship was an incentive to service and a precious solace in hours of suffering and imprisonment.

Thus, in the opening paragraphs of his epistle to the Philippians, he expresses his gratitude for all the joy he has found in the abiding loyalty of his Philippian friends. It was usual for him to begin his epistles with a thanksgiving. Where this was omitted, as in the letter to the Galatians, the omission was conspicuous and significant. Commonly this thanksgiving was for certain gifts or graces which the recipients of his letters were known to possess. In this letter, however, his gratitude is for his readers themselves. He rejoices in their sympathy, their love, and their constant kindness to him.

"I thank my God upon all my remembrance of you," he writes, thus naming another chief blessing of human life, namely, the power of memory. This faculty can be a treasure house out of which jewels may be drawn in hours of need. It can be a garden where fair flowers ever bloom. It has been said that "God gave us memory so that we might have roses in December."

Then, too, as in these words of the apostle, friendship

and memory may be united. It may be the recollection of
dear friends which gives to the day its brightness and its
cheer. This often is occasioned by a birthday celebration,
or by some expression at the opening of a new year, or by
some gift at Christmastide. So it was with Paul in his imprisonment. The memory of his friends in Philippi was
like the perfume of flowers wafted from a distant field.

So precious to him was this memory that for it he
thanked God. So dear to him were these friends that
whenever he prayed for them his petitions were offered
with gratitude and joy.

The particular time at which Paul called his friends to
mind was when he drew near to the throne of grace in
prayer. "Always in every supplication of mine" he specifies as the occasion of his thankful remembrance. In no
other way could his affection have been shown more truly
than by his prayers of intercession. Whenever memory
brought his friends to mind he lifted his heart to God for
them in petition; and whenever he bowed his knees in
prayer memory brought his friends before him.

The phrase "my God" indicates the intimate relation in
which Paul consciously stood with him whom he describes
as "the God whose I am, whom also I serve." The words
"all my remembrance of you" do not convey quite the
same idea as the other translation, "every remembrance of
you" (King James Version). The thought seems to be
that all the separate memories of the Philippian church,
taken together, formed one delightful, inspiring picture.
Such a picture when brought to mind enabled him to make
"supplication with joy."

The last word, "joy," sounds the keynote of the epistle.
Again and again through the passages which follow, this
glad note will be repeated. Paul will express his joy
though imprisoned, his joy when suffering opposition, his
joy even in the face of death. Here the joy is in prayer.

It is not often that prayer is pitched to the major key.
Usually our prayers are in a minor strain. Particularly is

this true of most public prayer. Possibly it is because inevitably there must be mention of much that is sad and distressing and tragic in our petitions for one another and for a troubled, suffering world. However, we should seek to follow more perfectly the example of the apostle, and to obey his precept, "In everything by prayer and supplication with thanksgiving let your requests be made known unto God."

Paul states to his friends in Philippi the specific occasion of his thanksgiving and joy. It is their "fellowship in furtherance of the gospel from the first day until now." They had shown themselves to be true missionaries by the sympathy and aid they had given him as he proclaimed the gospel. They had done so from the first day they heard the gospel, from the day when Lydia, accepting the message of salvation, received the messengers into her own home as guests, and from the day when as an infant church they sent aid to Paul after he had left them and had reached Thessalonica. From these first acts of kindness, years before, down to this very time when relief had been sent him in Rome by the hand of Epaphroditus, they had been partakers in forwarding the great work of evangelizing the world. Thus Paul is rejoicing in the fact that those who remain at home and give of their substance to support the missionary have a real and substantial part in his work and will some day share his reward.

However, the "fellowship" of the Philippians "in furtherance of the gospel" is not to be confined in its meaning to the material support they had given to Paul, but it includes their sympathy, their prayers, and their definite witness for Christ in their own church; in fact, it denotes all they had been and done as "saints in Christ Jesus" at Philippi.

In view of all the faithful service which these friends have rendered, Paul expresses his confident belief that they will continue in the same fruitful activity until the day when Christ returns. This confidence is based, however, not so much on the fidelity of man as on the grace and purpose and faithfulness of God, "being confident of this very thing, that he who began a good work in you will perfect it until the day of Jesus Christ" (v. 6).

The "good work" may refer to their reception of the gospel and their faithful fellowship in its promotion and advance; or it may denote the spiritual life which expressed itself in such sympathetic labor and effort. Thus the "work" may be that of sanctification or of service. However, in view of the connection with what has just been stated and with what follows, it probably refers not to the perfecting of character so much as to the furtherance of the gospel. Paul is confident that God, who has begun in them this "work" will continue it until Christ again appears. This "day" of his appearing will be the time when the task is complete. Until then, the "gospel of the kingdom . . . [must] be preached in the whole world for a testimony unto all the nations."

Paul justifies his joyful confidence in the Philippians on the ground of his loving regard for them as participants with him in the grace of God. "Even as it is right for me to be thus minded on behalf of you all," he writes, "because I have you in my heart, inasmuch as, both in my bonds and in the defence and confirmation of the gospel, ye all are partakers with me of grace." (V. 7.)

Paul holds them in his "heart," not only in his affection—which he emphasizes in the verse which follows—but in his thought, in his loving remembrance, in his belief. He knows them to be sharers with him of the same divine grace which enables him to labor for Christ. This grace is unfailing and inexhaustible. By it the work begun in them will be perfected "until the day of Jesus Christ." He is sure that this will be true of them since they have shown themselves to be united with him in closest fellowship, both in his sufferings and in his witness for Christ.

His "defence" may refer to his trial before the Roman magistrates, as the term is often used in a judicial and technical sense. Probably it should not be so limited. It rather refers to the negative side of all Paul's preaching as "confirmation" indicates its positive side. Thus in all the labors of the apostle, as well as in his trials, his Philippian friends have been united with him and have shared with him in the grace of God. This fellowship has been manifested in their remembrance of Paul in his "bonds," and in all their efforts for the defense and furtherance of the gospel.

His confidence as to their future is thus fully justified by his love for them, as for those who share the grace given him of God. How deep that love is Paul indicates by an affirmation so emphatic as to take the form of a solemn oath: "For God is my witness, how I long after you all in the tender mercies of Christ Jesus." Paul thus speaks of his love as though it were identical with the love of Christ. He loves his friends with the very heart of Christ. With that heart his own beats in unison. Paul is so truly one with his Master as to affirm that his personal longing for his friends in Philippi is inseparable from the love of Christ for them.

This precious paragraph in which Paul expresses his joyful gratitude for his Christian companions indicates that the strongest bonds of friendship are those which are formed by fellowship in Christian service. There are other ties by which hearts are united. Some are sentimental and emotional. Some are due to common interests and sympathies and mental attitudes. However, those which are the most sacred and abiding are those which are due to a common relationship with Christ, and to an earnest co-operation in work undertaken for his sake. The aged prisoner in Rome could call God to witness his devoted love for friends in distant Philippi who, from the first day of their acquaintance, had labored and sacrificed with him in furtherance of the gospel of Christ.

Then again, this glowing paragraph reminds us that all friendships need to be purified and can be glorified by the power of Christ. Much that is selfish and unworthy is often mistaken for love. When, however, one realizes the love of Christ, when one seeks to know the mind of Christ, when one is submissive to the will of Christ, then human affections are ennobled and strengthened until they partake of the very holiness and passion which flow from the heart of Christ himself.

C. THE PRAYER   Ch. 1:9-11

9 And this I pray, that your love may abound yet more and more in knowledge and all discernment; 10 so that ye may approve the things that are excellent; that ye may be sincere and void of offence unto the day of Christ; 11 being filled with the fruits of righteousness, which are through Jesus Christ, unto the glory and praise of God.

Paul usually opens each of his epistles with a salutation, a thanksgiving, and a prayer. In some cases the notes of praise and prayer are blended. Here the thanksgiving and the petition are kept distinct, but they are closely united. Paul's gratitude has been expressed for the friendship and cooperation of the Christians in Philippi; he now remembers these friends in prayer. In voicing his gratitude he has intimated that he prays for them frequently; he now gives the substance of his prayer. In stating his thankfulness for their fellowship he has solemnly affirmed that his affection for them is one with the tenderness and love of Christ; he now prays that their love may be made perfect by the power of Christ.

It is ever true that we can render to our friends no greater service than by praying for them; and we here are reminded further that friendships in no way can be more elevated and safeguarded than by prayer.

Paul does not pray that his Philippian friends may have love for one another and for him. He knows that such love already exists. He is familiar with their warmhearted and ardent affection. Its recent manifestation toward him is the very occasion of this letter. He does not ask that the full tide of love may be stayed, but that it may be confined to right channels and may be kept free from all that is selfish and impure.

There is a definite progress in his thought. First he asks that love may abound in the power of correct moral choice, and then that such choice may result in high character, and then that this character may be manifested in good works, which finally will redound to the glory and praise of God.

First of all, then, his prayer is, "That your love may abound yet more and more in knowledge and all discernment." By "knowledge" he indicates the possession of right moral principles, and "discernment" denotes the ability to apply these principles to specific circumstances and cases. This term "knowledge" is a favorite with Paul. It is particularly prominent in the prayers of his imprisonment. It denotes a full knowledge, a practical knowledge, an experimental knowledge, and that quite definitely in the moral and spiritual realm. "Discernment" is the faculty of moral sensibility and spiritual perception. It implies a sensitive conscience, a delicacy of ethical tact, and a clear moral insight. Thus Paul prays that love may grow richer and richer in these two respects, accurate knowledge of right and alertness in applying such knowledge to the experiences of life.

Nothing is more needed today. Men are insisting that there are no fixed moral standards, that right and wrong are merely relative terms, that natural desires are to determine conduct, and that free expression of self is to be the controlling principle of life. Quite on the contrary, Paul insists that we are not to be the creatures of circumstance; nor are we to be ruled by impulse and desire. Love must itself be wise and discriminating. It is not to be confused with unregulated and selfish passion. It is not to be blinded by false reasoning. It should abound in "knowledge" and all "discernment."

Such love will enable one to "approve the things that are excellent," or, as otherwise translated, to "distinguish the things that differ." The sense is much the same. In either case the result in view is the approval of the choice of that which is good. Paul is emphasizing the need of wise and careful discrimination. Circumstances are continually arising which present difficult moral problems. There are common practices which the conscience of one Christian will allow and the conscience of another Christian will forbid. One must be guarded, on the one hand, against being morally lax and, on the other, against being over-scrupulous. Love, if wise and morally sensitive, will enable a man to choose aright even in cases which involve delicate but necessary distinctions between courses and acts as to whether they are right or wrong.

As a result of such careful discrimination in the matter of moral choice, Christians may be "sincere and void of offence." The origin of the word translated "sincere" is difficult to ascertain. "Judged in the sunlight" is a familiar and attractive but hardly accurate rendering. The idea of "purity" seems inherent in the term as commonly used. It may possibly be taken to mean "transparency of character," or "perfect openness towards God." Then by way of contrast "void of offence" may denote "giving no offense to others." Thus both the terms together may denote a life which is rightly related both to God and to men.

Beyond all question the two terms describe a character which can stand the test of divine judgment. Such is the meaning of Paul when he prays that his readers "may be sincere and void of offence unto the day of Christ." This "day" is that when "we must all be made manifest before the judgment-seat of Christ." It is the day when we shall receive his final approval and reward. It is with this in view, with the thought of being prepared for his coming, that Christians are to be "sincere and void of offence."

This return of Christ was with Paul an unfailing source

of comfort and of hope, and a constant incentive and inspiration to right living and to faithful service. However, he refers to the event with marked sanity and reserve. He never attempts to determine the date for the coming of Christ. In no place does he affirm that it will be in his own lifetime. In some of his writings he identifies himself in thought with those who will be alive when Christ returns. (I Thess. 4:15.) In other places he identifies himself with believers who will die before the coming of Christ. (II Cor. 4:14.) In this letter to the Philippians he regards his own death as imminent rather than the return of his Lord. In a later letter he is certain that he will not live until the coming of Christ. (II Tim. 4:6.) However, this great event is to encourage Timothy to diligent effort. Thus in this letter to the Philippians, Paul mentions the "day" of Jesus Christ, first (ch. 1:6), as the time when faithful service will be complete, and here as the time when holy living will receive its reward (v. 10). His reference to "the day of Christ," as he writes here to the Philippians, is much like the exhortation of John so to abide in Christ that when he appears we shall have confidence "and not be ashamed before him at his coming" (I John 2:28), and it is with this thought in mind that Paul prays for the Philippians that they "may be sincere and void of offence unto the day of Christ."

Such pure and faultless character will naturally express itself in deeds of helpfulness and service. Thus in his prayer Paul adds the more positive aspect of the picture: "Filled with the fruits of righteousness, which are through Jesus Christ." The "fruits of righteousness" are the fruits which righteousness produces. "Righteousness" indicates a true relation to God made possible by faith, and then denotes, as in this verse, that moral uprightness and that holy activity which result in a harvest of good works. Fruitful lives should be the visible outcome of wise and discerning love. This is the very purpose of the apostle's prayer.

However, fruitfulness is possible only by union with

Christ.   Just as it is understood that the sensitive moral judgments and discriminations for which Paul prays are possible only by the power of the indwelling Spirit, so, as here expressed, fruitfulness in life and service is dependent upon the power of Christ and upon a continual abiding in him.   All the "fruits of righteousness" are "through Jesus Christ."

They are also "unto the glory and praise of God."   This is the purpose and end of the fruitage for which Paul prays.   "Glory" means "manifested excellence."   When referred to God it often signifies the revelation of his redeeming grace.   When Christians show toward one another a love which, while fervent, is at the same time wise and discriminating, when their choices develop into characters which are transparent and free from offense, when their lives are rich in the "fruits of righteousness," then God is glorified, for such transformed human lives are a demonstration of divine power.   Every loving, pure, and fruitful Christian life is a witness to the redeeming grace of God.

The final result is the "praise of God," for "praise" is the recognition by men of the "glory" which has been manifested.   They render to God homage and honor in view of the power and grace revealed in the lives of the redeemed.

Such seems to be the burden of the prayer offered by Paul the prisoner for his friends in the Philippian church.   It is a form of supplication which might well be upon the lips of all who long for the advancement of the cause of Christ.

II
PAUL'S EXPERIENCE IN ROME
Ch. 1:12-26

A. IMPRISONED AND OPPOSED   Ch. 1:12-20

12 Now I would have you know, brethren, that the things which happened *unto me have fallen out rather unto the progress of the gospel; 13 so that my bonds became manifest in Christ throughout the whole prætorian guard, and to all the rest; 14 and that most of the brethren in the Lord, being confident through my bonds, are more abundantly bold to speak the word of God without fear. 15 Some indeed preach Christ even of envy and strife; and some also of good will: 16 the one* do it *of love, knowing that I am set for the defence of the gospel; 17 but the other proclaim Christ of faction, not sincerely, thinking to raise up affliction for me in my bonds. 18 What then? only that in every way, whether in pretence or in truth, Christ is proclaimed; and therein I rejoice, yea, and will rejoice. 19 For I know that this shall turn out to my salvation, through your supplication and the supply of the Spirit of Jesus Christ, 20 according to my earnest expectation and hope, that in nothing shall I be put to shame, but that with all boldness, as always, so now also Christ shall be magnified in my body, whether by life, or by death.*

In his opening thanksgiving and prayer, Paul has poured out his love for his friends in Philippi. As he now enters upon the main portion of his letter it is natural that he should tell his readers something of his own situation and experiences in Rome. He knew of their love. They had expressed that in their gifts. He was sure that they would be eager, first of all, to hear of his welfare. Indeed, letters had come indicating that they knew of the illness of their messenger, Epaphroditus, and most probably they had in-

dicated the deep concern they felt for Paul himself. With
the generosity of love he mentions nothing that would
distress the minds of his friends. He assures them that all
is well, indeed that all things are working together for
good, and that his heart is full of joy and of hope.

Paul was a prisoner. As to the place and nature of his
confinement there are differences of view. Due weight
should be given to the words of Luke: "And when we
entered into Rome, Paul was suffered to abide by himself
with the soldier that guarded him. . . . And he abode
two whole years in his own hired dwelling, and received
all that went in unto him, preaching the kingdom of God,
and teaching the things concerning the Lord Jesus Christ
with all boldness, none forbidding him." Evidently as a
prisoner of distinction, reserved for the personal judgment
of the emperor, and charged with no crime or felony, he
was accorded a large degree of liberty and certain real
courtesies.

There are those, however, who conjecture that the period
of advantage had passed; that this letter was written near
the end of the "two whole years"; and that Paul had been
transferred from his private lodging to the stricter custody
of the prison, where those were confined who were awaiting trial.

Even the more lenient and less rigorous imprisonment
must have been distressing to Paul. To be chained to the
wrist of a rude soldier, day and night, sleeping or wak-
ing, must have been a trying experience to one of Paul's
sensitive disposition. Then, in addition to his physical
discomfort, there must have been much to embitter and to
distress him. To a man of his tireless activity the restrictions of imprisonment must have been intolerable. He
was eager to visit the churches he had founded. He had
planned to continue his adventurous evangelistic tours as
far westward as Spain. In fact he had expected to preach
the gospel throughout all the empire of Rome. How narrow then must have seemed those walls by which he was

confined! How small his audiences! How unlike those at Corinth or at Athens!

Then, too, there was the long delay of justice. Month after month dragged by and his trial was still postponed. And what was the issue of that trial to be? What was to be expected at the judgment seat of a Nero?

However, as Paul now addresses himself to his dear friends in Philippi there is not a word of bitterness or complaint. His physical conditions are not so distressing as when years before he lay beaten and bleeding in the dank dungeon at Philippi. His mental trials are as great. Yet as he then sang songs in the night, so he now breaks forth in a hymn of joy. He is expressing the experience, not merely of a prisoner in Rome, but of a man who is "in Christ Jesus."

His first reason for rejoicing is that the very fact of his imprisonment is making the gospel more widely known. "Now I would have you know, brethren," he writes, "that the things which happened unto me have fallen out rather unto the progress of the gospel." By "the things which happened" he means his experiences as a prisoner. His friends might have imagined that this event had put an end to Paul's gospel ministry. He declares that, on the contrary, it "rather" had furthered the preaching of the "good tidings." He explains how this can be: "My bonds became manifest in Christ throughout the whole prætorian guard, and to all the rest." That is, it had become known that he was in bonds because of no crime but merely because he was a Christian. His very imprisonment, therefore, had led men to know and to discuss the story of Christ. It had become in itself a means and an occasion of making the gospel known, and that, too, in wide and unexpected circles. These circles included "the whole prætorian guard."

The word so rendered is possibly the most debated term in the entire epistle. Does it mean the soldiers who formed the Praetorian Guard, or the barracks or camp of this guard, or the palace of the emperor or ruler, or the judges and officials of the imperial court? Probably the first translation is to be preferred. Paul was to be tried before the tribunal of the emperor. It was natural, therefore, that he should be committed to the charge of the praetorian troops which formed the imperial guard. This guard numbered some ten thousand picked men. Originally they were drawn from Italy but later from other parts of the empire, including Macedonia and Spain. They were granted special privileges, double wages, and, when retiring, a liberal bounty. Soldiers from these troops, apparently, were detailed one after another to guard Paul in his private dwelling.

These rude legionaries might have been regarded as unwelcome associates by the refined and cultured apostle; but he looked upon each one in succession as a possible messenger of Christ. One can almost imagine the surprise, the disdain, and then the deepening interest with which these soldiers overheard the strange teachings of their prisoner. They listened to his conversation with men of all classes who came to his room, to his discussions with excited Jews, to his conferences with friends, to letters which he dictated to distant churches; and then in the long hours of dreary nights they heard the true Way set forth so winsomely, so passionately, that one after another was led to enlist as a soldier of Christ and go forth to win from him a crown.

Gradually the report of the apostle and his message spread through all the guard, and beyond them "to all the rest" in Rome. Not that everyone heard the "good news," but it was talked of throughout the whole city, and even some members "of Cæsar's household" were won to the Christian faith.

Such a surprising result of his imprisonment was the first fact mentioned by the apostle to relieve the anxiety of his friends and to explain his own comfort and joy.

There was a second. This was the fact that his presence

in Rome, and the way he was improving the very opportunities of his imprisonment, had given new courage and strength to the Christians of the Imperial City. "Most of the brethren in the Lord," he writes, "being confident through my bonds, are more abundantly bold to speak the word of God without fear."

There is a contagion of courage and passion. This helpless prisoner, shut off from the work he loved, confined to his obscure lodging, spread new zeal and fiery devotion throughout the whole church of Rome. Some Christians may have lost heart. Some may have been failing in their witness. Some may have been unfaithful to their Lord. However, when they saw how Paul bore his bonds, they began anew their fearless testimony for Christ.

In connection with this new and wider preaching by the Christians of Rome came an experience which would have daunted a more timid soul but which Paul mentions as a third, and indeed as the specific, occasion for his joy. This was the opposition on the part of certain members of the church.

"Some indeed preach Christ even of envy and strife," he writes. They "proclaim Christ of faction, not sincerely, thinking to raise up affliction for me in my bonds." It is commonly supposed that these were the Judaizers, who everywhere dogged Paul's footsteps and tried to bind upon his converts the burden of the Mosaic law. However, Paul does not appear to be concerned here with those who taught false doctrines or "another gospel," but with those who taught the true gospel while inspired with wrong motives.

Just who they were we are left to conjecture. Possibly they came from the Jewish element in the Roman church. Obviously they were envious of Paul. They were moved by personal jealousy and sought to undermine his influence. They sought to form a faction in the church. They were indeed so moved by malice that they would gladly have added to the distress of Paul's imprisonment.

It is not difficult to imagine men of this kind. Judaizers

were not the only men to disturb the early church.   Teachers exist today who set forth sound doctrine but are animated by jealousy and ill will.   They "proclaim Christ of faction."   In their rivalry and contentiousness they even aim to bring bitterness into the lives of their fellow workers and divisions into the body of Christ.

There were others.   They preached Christ "of good will" and "of love."   They supported and furthered the work of Paul as of one who was divinely appointed to proclaim and defend the gospel.   They loved Paul because he preached the good tidings which they themselves were setting forth.

The attitude toward those who were seeking to oppose and offend him is an inspiring revelation of the greatness of the mind and heart of the apostle.   He might have criticized and rebuked them.   He might have let those Roman soldiers learn with contempt how Christian preachers can be lacking in love.   But Paul rises above any petty animosity or personal pique.   He seizes upon the main fact, namely, that Christ is being preached, and instead of resentment his heart is filled with joy.

"What then?" he asks.   What difference does it make? In either case, whether motives be false or pure, "whether in pretence or in truth, Christ is proclaimed."   That is the important thing.   Nothing else matters.   The gospel is being preached, "and therein I rejoice."

There is something superb in this tolerant attitude of the apostle.   It is a tolerance born not of indifference but of a burning zeal for Christ.   Paul does not rejoice in wrong motives, in "faction" and "pretence," but in the fact that in spite of the imperfections in the preachers the gospel is being preached.

Paul was large enough to seize upon the salient point in the situation.   He did not trouble himself too greatly about the aims and errors and faults of other men.   Above all their contending voices he heard the name of Christ.   With all that was false and unkind in their preaching, he caught the great notes of the glorious gospel.   No matter what

was in their hearts the gospel was on their lips. By friend
and foe alike that gospel was being proclaimed in Rome.
Therein Paul rejoiced.

His joy was to continue. Nothing could quench it, for
there was a fourth aspect of his present experience which
filled him with comfort and delight. "I rejoice, yea, and
will rejoice," he writes. "For I know that this shall turn
out to my salvation." Paul was confident that his imprisonment and all its attendant circumstances would result in his highest good.

By his "salvation" Paul must have meant much more
than release from imprisonment, for it is to be experienced
either in death or in life. The word has much the same
meaning as when Paul writes, "Work out your own salvation with fear and trembling" (ch. 2:12), and again, "God
chose you from the beginning unto salvation in sanctification of the Spirit and belief of the truth" (II Thess. 2:13).
Paul is sure that his present troubles, his imprisonment
and the personal antagonisms of his adversaries, will result in his spiritual development and so in his truest
welfare.

This blessed result, however, is conditioned on the
prayers of his friends and the agency of the Holy Spirit.
It is to be, as Paul writes, "through your supplication and
the supply of the Spirit of Jesus Christ." As the love of
Paul has led him to make intercession for the Philippians,
so he takes it for granted that they will make "supplication" for him. Then, too, he realizes that the sanctifying
issue of his trials can be secured only by the influence of
the Spirit of God, whom Paul here, as elsewhere, identifies
with the "Spirit of Jesus Christ."

This spiritual development Paul further declares to be
in absolute accord with the supreme aim of his life. It
will be in fulfillment of his "earnest expectation and hope,"
which is that he never shall have reason to feel ashamed,
but that "as always, so now," with the uncertain issue of his
trial before him, he may act and speak with all courage,

so that Christ will be honored in his body "whether by life, or by death." Paul says "in my body," rather than "in me" or "in my person," because he is facing uncertainty of physical life or death. If he lives, he hopes to honor Christ by his continued service and testimony; if he must die, then by his dauntless courage he will do credit to his divine Lord.

Such were Paul's "uses of adversity." Thus in his time of trial he showed the triumph of his faith. First, he employed his irksome imprisonment as an occasion for making Christ known throughout the Imperial City. Thus, too, the servants of Christ in all ages, confined in gloomy jails, shut in by blindness, held captive by bodily suffering, have sent forth messages of hope and cheer which have been the gladness of the world. The time of limitation is often the time of opportunity.

Secondly, his distresses were so cheerfully endured that he gave courage to an entire church. Thus the witness of fortitude exerts its unconscious influence and enables fellow soldiers to advance with firmer tread and with fearless hearts.

Further still, broad-minded tolerance and passionate devotion to the things which are vital delivered the apostle, as they deliver Christians today, from bitterness of soul, from anger and ill will.

Lastly, here was a man who believed that disappointments and hardships, in the case of those who are sustained by the Spirit of God, may be used for the perfecting of character and for the glory of Christ. Paul knew that "to them that love God all things work together for good."

B. IN THE FACE OF DEATH   Ch. 1:21-26

21 For to me to live is Christ, and to die is gain. 22 But if to live in the flesh,—if this shall bring fruit from my work, then what I shall choose I know not. 23 But I am in a strait betwixt the two, having the desire to depart and be with Christ; for it is very far better: 24 yet to abide in the flesh is more needful for your sake. 25 And having this confidence, I know that I shall abide, yea, and abide with you all, for your progress and joy in the faith; 26 that your glorying my abound in Christ Jesus in me through my presence with you again.

Paul had a profound philosophy of life. It was expressed in a single comprehensive phrase, "For to me to live is Christ." The aim, the purpose, the inspiration, the sum of his life was Christ. In some measure the same can be true of all Christians. Such a view gives to life a real unity and a true nobility. It ends those conflicting aims, those divided allegiances, which destroy all harmony, which make efforts fruitless and fill life with those activities which are at once complex and futile. Such a philosophy also dignifies all one may do or may endure. When tasks are undertaken for the sake of Christ they are ennobled, no matter how obscure they may be. When distress is endured patiently by the power of Christ the very experience has about it something of joy.

There was, however, one phase of life which Paul had specially in mind. He was referring in particular to the service of Christ, to public witness for Christ, to proclaiming the gospel of Christ. He had just spoken of his supreme aim and purpose: to testify for Christ with such unfailing courage as always to reflect glory upon the name of his Lord. He is about to say that, if he is to live longer, it will be with the one hope of being fruitful in his work for Christ and helpful to the followers of Christ. So here he is saying that for him the supreme aim, the inclusive experience in life, is to make Christ known.

There is something emphatic about the phrase "To me." Whatever may be true of others, this he knows to be true of himself. There are, indeed, countless others of whom it is not true. The common goals of life are strangely contrasted with the single purpose of Paul. Men commonly struggle for wealth and fame, for power and pleasure and gratification of self, and many of them struggle hopelessly and with bitter hearts. Paul differs even from those who live with unselfish purpose and according to high standards of endeavor, in that his activities are determined not by mere principles but by his relation to a divine Person. Principles may be good, even admirable, but they are cold and powerless in comparison with conscious devotion to the living Christ.

There is another possible reason for the emphasis Paul expresses in referring to himself. In explaining to his readers his experience in prison he has just intimated that his testimony for Christ may reach its climax in a martyr's death. To his friends the mere suggestion would bring distress. He would reassure them by stating that, in his own view, life is summed up and has found its purpose and meaning in fearless witness for Christ. Therefore he cries exultantly, "For to me to live is Christ, and to die is gain."

In his estimation death was nothing to cause distress or sorrow or fear. Just because "to live is Christ," therefore "to die is gain," for it will bring one into an even more precious relationship to Christ; it will be "to depart and be with Christ." The fellowship with Christ which makes life so blessed will then be complete; the service which is now the supreme purpose and privilege of life will then assume more glorious forms; the knowledge of Christ which is the chief joy of life will then be made perfect. Paul does not mean that "to die is gain" because it will bring an end to pain and sorrow and toil, but because it will bring more of Christ; it will make possible the full enjoyment of those "unsearchable riches of Christ" which are now known only in part. Paul does not mean that "to die is gain" because life is so intolerable, but because death issues in what is so desirable. It will give in fuller measure that which is now the very essence and glory of life.

Such is Paul's conclusion when he considers the comparative advantages of life and death for himself; but it is not with a view to himself alone that such a possibility is to be faced. He must think of others, and of the relation which a continuance of his life work may sustain to them. This also must be considered if a choice between life and death is to be expressed. The desire for death may be selfish; it may be cowardly; it may be unchristian.

"But if to live in the flesh," Paul ponders, "if this shall bring fruit from my work, then what I shall choose I know not." He speaks of life "in the flesh," because, when man has left his body of flesh and blood, he will still live, and live indeed more fully and more really. Paul assumes that his continued life in the flesh will result in "fruit" from his "work," that is, in the gospel preached, in souls saved, in "saints" strengthened. With that assured, shall he choose to live or choose to die? He is in doubt: "What I shall choose I know not." He cannot tell.

He admits that he is in a dilemma: "Having the desire to depart and be with Christ; for it is very far better: yet to abide in the flesh is more needful for your sake."

Paul cannot tell whether to choose life or death. There are strong reasons for either choice. "I am in a strait betwixt the two," he declares. He is in a "narrow" place, on a narrow road. He is between two walls. He cannot move in either direction. He is held motionless. Pressure comes from both sides, from the considerations that he has mentioned which might determine his choice of life or death.

On the one hand, he admits a real longing for what death will bring: "Having the desire to depart and be with Christ; for it is very far better." That is his view of death. It is a departure to "be with Christ." The word "depart" means to "unloose." It pictures a ship being unloosed from its moorings, or the loosing of tent pins for breaking camp. If Paul used the word in a figurative sense, he probably had the latter picture in mind. He rarely used figures drawn from the sea or from nautical life. He was surrounded by soldiers and frequently employed military terms. Possibly he means to describe death as the striking of a tent in preparation for a last short journey. We may indeed thus translate his words to the Corinthians: "For we know that if the mere tent of our bodily frame, which is our earthly dwelling, is taken down, we have in heaven a house built not by human hands but by God, which will abide forever." Death so described, as the taking down of a tent, may indicate that one final day's march is to be taken which will bring the pilgrim out of the wilderness and across the river and into the city of gold.

It is not, in any case, upon the experience of dying that Paul fixes his thought, but upon that which follows death. Death may be a departure, but it is the destination which makes Paul yearn to go. The way may be forbidding, but it is "a short dark passage to eternal light." "To depart" is to "be with Christ." This for the Christian is the issue of death. This is the essence of glory. Such should be the confidence of everyone who falls asleep in the Christian faith. "To be absent from the body" is "to be at home with the Lord." Not much more need be said. This is not sufficient to satisfy our curiosity; it is sufficient for our comfort. Our gaze longingly follows those loved ones who have joined the great caravan for the last journey; we wonder where they are abiding. This much we know: They have gone to "be with Christ" and this we know "is very far better."

All that it means to "be with Christ" we can only faintly conjecture. It must denote conscious blessedness, the "vision beatific," perfect communion with Christ, unbroken fellowship with him, participation in his divine glory. At the very least, Paul knew that for himself it would be an experience far better than the very best of life.

On the other hand, Paul cannot overlook what his death or life will mean to his friends and converts. It is with no false pride or self-consciousness that he writes, "Yet to abide in the flesh is more needful for your sake." He knows how absolutely they are dependent upon his sympathy, his counsel, his guidance, and his prayers. His eagerness to meet their need outweighs his desire for personal gain. He prefers to live and to labor on. Paul was not a man who wished to die before his work was done or while he saw any needful duty to be performed. He was not one to shirk his task on earth that he might find rest in heaven.

In view of what he may be to his friends, his great choice is made. Indeed there comes to his mind, not only a willingness either to live or to die, but a deep conviction that he is to live and to continue his blessed ministry for the "saints" at Philippi. "And having this confidence," he writes, "I know that I shall abide, yea, and abide with you all."

No one can fail to notice the true nobleness of Paul's decision and desire. It is not the choice of one who wishes to live because he is afraid to die, nor of one who wishes to die because he lacks the courage to live. In his soliloquy he does not answer the question, "To be, or not to be," by choosing the ills he has rather than fly to others that he knows not of. Nor is he so weary of life with its burdens, its shocks, and its heartaches, that he idly dreams of the bliss that lies beyond the "sleep of death."

Of the sorrows of life he has had his full share. For him to depart woul be "very far better." Yet in view of the service he can render to his friends he manfully girds himself for his task. He feels certain that he is to live, and to live in helpful fellowship with them "all." It is to be a fellowship which will promote their spiritual advancement and their Christian joy. Or, as he says, "I shall abide . . . for your progress and joy in the faith."

More specifically this progress and joy are to consist in the fresh ground for Christian exultation which they will have in Paul when he is restored to them again. This, then, is the ultimate aim of his abiding in the flesh, and in fellowship with his friends, as he states it in his own words: "That your glorying may abound in Christ Jesus in me through my presence with you again." Their "glorying," their pride, their ground for boasting, is to be "in Christ" who is its sphere. It is to be related to him and his gospel and his work. However, the immediate occasion of this "glorying" will be Paul. He will be its special cause and, more particularly still, the "glorying" will be on account of his personal presence with them again.

In such lofty terms does Paul express his joyful anticipation of being restored to his Philippian friends. The statement of confident hope forms the climax of his message concerning his personal experiences in Rome. He is a prisoner, yet his imprisonment is an occasion for making the gospel widely known. His presence is encouraging others in their witness for Christ. Even his enemies are preaching the gospel with more zeal. His own spiritual life is being deepened by all that is befalling him. He is confident that his trial before the emperor is to have a happy issue and he is to rejoin his friends. It is such a view of his circumstances that enables Paul to rejoice and to transform the place of his imprisonment into a house of praise.

III
PRACTICAL EXHORTATIONS
Chs. 1:27 to 2:18

A. TO STEADFASTNESS   Ch. 1:27-30

27 Only let your manner of life be worthy of the gospel of Christ: that, whether I come and see you or be absent, I may hear of your state, that ye stand fast in one spirit, with one soul striving for the faith of the gospel; 28 and in nothing affrighted by the adversaries: which is for them an evident token of perdition, but of your salvation, and that from God; 29 because to you it hath been granted in the behalf of Christ, not only to believe on him, but also to suffer in his behalf: 30 having the same conflict which ye saw in me, and now hear to be in me.

Paul has just stated his confident hope that his imprisonment will end and that he will enjoy the privilege of visiting again his friends in Philippi. However, his trial before the emperor had not yet been brought to an issue, and no one could be sure what Caesar might do. At best, the decision was being delayed. Paul was not yet free. As Epaphroditus was now leaving for Philippi it was necessary for Paul to content himself with writing. He therefore urges his friends to continue in their consistent Christian life.

If he comes to Philippi, as he hopes to do, his purpose will be to further the spiritual progress of his friends and to increase their joy. This purpose can be secured, or, pending his arrival, this "progress and joy" can be maintained, only on the condition that they are steadfast in their loyalty to Christ.

Therefore, under any circumstances, whether he is to come to Philippi or whether he is to be detained longer in

Rome, he exhorts them to conduct themselves in a manner worthy of their Christian profession.

"Only let your manner of life be worthy of the gospel of Christ." These words may be rendered more literally, "Only behave as citizens worthily of the gospel of Christ." It is not certain, however, that in the time of Paul the term "behave as citizens" still retained its literal meaning. The reference to living in a community seems to have gradually been lost and the term came to mean merely "live."

Scholars, however, have always been eager to find here at least some trace of the original significance, which indeed is quite obvious in a similar term, which Paul uses later on when he says, "Our citizenship is in heaven." Here it may be possible to discern at least a shade of meaning still surviving from the original use of the word, indicating a life ordered by certain fixed rules or laws, like that of citizens in a commonwealth or state.

For a Christian the rule or law of his life is that it should be "worthy of the gospel of Christ." The colonists in Philippi were controlled by the Roman code. As Christians they had regulations to observe that were just as definite and binding as the laws of the Imperial City. The gospel is not merely a message to be believed; it is a rule to be obeyed. It does not consist merely in dogmas and doctrines to be discussed and debated and arranged in a system; it embodies vital principles which regulate the conscience and determine right conduct. It is "the gospel of Christ." It points to him as the Lord of life. His will is set forth as sovereign and supreme. His grace is promised as sufficient to supply every need, and to overcome every weakness. "The gospel of Christ," therefore, sets one free from minute and vexatious requirements and restrictions. It provides a great unifying and liberating principle, namely, that of submission to Christ and faith in him. One who seeks to live "worthily of the gospel of Christ" is not controlled by the maxims and judgments of men. He is not satisfied with popular codes of morality.

While engaged in the humblest tasks on earth, he is living as a citizen of heaven.

Paul urges the Philippians so to live that if he is present he may observe in them such conduct or if he is absent he may hear a favorable report of them. He does not wish their behavior to be regulated by the mere accident of the presence or absence of a friend. Unfortunately, much human conduct is so determined. One course of action is followed in the presence of certain persons and quite another in their absence. Paul here enjoins upon his friends a consistent manner of life. "That, whether I come and see you or be absent, I may hear of your state," he writes, and then at once specifies the character of that "state" or conduct of which he hopes to learn.

It is to be marked by moral steadfastness, and a steadfastness which is at once united and undaunted. It is to be united in its relation to fellow Christians. It is to be undaunted in the face of foes. The Philippians are to "stand fast in one spirit." The reference here is not to the Holy Spirit, but to that disposition, that character, that moral temper which the Holy Spirit creates. This disposition should be manifested by the same mental and spiritual attitude, being of "one soul." These Christians should be one in heart and mind. They further should be "striving" together "for the faith of the gospel." Like fellow athletes they should stand shoulder to shoulder, defending and advancing that faith in Christ which the gospel teaches and inspires.

This unity of life and effort Paul further emphasizes in a paragraph which follows. Indeed, to enforce such unity is one of the aims of this epistle. Here, however, he lays more particular stress upon the steadfast courage which his readers should manifest. "In nothing affrighted by the adversaries" is the phrase by which he describes their proper attitude.

"Affrighted" describes those who are suddenly terrified or intimidated, as by the unexpected appearance of opposition or the sudden attack of an enemy. It describes many Christians today. Their faith seems to be swept away by the first breath of antagonism or of criticism. A single book, or one pronouncement of a self-confident skeptic, overthrows the convictions of a lifetime, or at least produces a spiritual paralysis which makes active effort for Christ impossible. The adversaries of the present day are nothing in comparison with those which opposed the believers in Philippi or attacked Paul in Rome. However, they are sufficiently strong and terrifying. Confident courage and calm assurance in the face of such opposition indicate a source of divine strength. They are, therefore, a proof that those who reveal such calmness are on the side of God and under his protection and care. They are also a proof, or evidence, or "evident token of perdition," of that loss of eternal life, of that destruction, which must await all the enemies of God.

Of this spiritual ruin of their adversaries the courageous conduct of the Philippians is an evident and unmistakable token. On the other hand, their brave bearing is a proof and assurance of their own eternal safety. For their courage is an indication that they are united with Christ, and their union with Christ makes certain their salvation. This proof, or evident token, is "from God." It is in accordance with a divine arrangement or provision. It is further shown by the fact of their being permitted to be united in their sufferings with Christ, indeed of being allowed to suffer for Christ's sake, or "in the behalf of Christ." This is a further proof of their union with Christ, a union which assures salvation.

Paul even intimates that this suffering is a privilege. It is something granted in and by the grace of God, "because to you it hath been granted in the behalf of Christ, not only to believe on him, but also to suffer in his behalf."

It is no privilege to suffer, but it may be a privilege to suffer for Christ's sake, to suffer when one is certain that his sufferings are not due to his own fault or error but are wholly for the sake of Christ and for the advancement of his cause. No one should court suffering, but, when it comes, possibly it may be endured in such a spirit as to advance the cause of Christ; and suffering endured in his cause may be regarded as a gift or arrangement of God's grace.

As a specific instance of such suffering, Paul is able to refer to his own case, and to assure the Philippians that their experience is one with his, "having the same conflict which ye saw in me, and now hear to be in me." They had seen Paul at Philippi. There he had been beaten and imprisoned for the sake of Christ. Now they are hearing from Epaphroditus of Paul's imprisonment and hardships in Rome. However, these Philippians, in their present sufferings, can have the encouragement and comfort of knowing that they have a part with the heroic old athlete in the glorious conflict he is waging for Christ and his gospel. In that conflict they all can be victorious. As they now share in Paul's struggle, they can be sure that each one who continues faithful and unafraid now in the face of the enemy will receive at his Lord's return the victor's imperishable crown.

B. TO UNITY   Ch. 2:1-4

1 If there is therefore any exhortation in Christ, if any consolation of love, if any fellowship of the Spirit, if any tender mercies and compassions, 2 make full my joy, that ye be of the same mind, having the same love, being of one accord, of one mind; 3 doing nothing through faction or through vainglory, but in lowliness of mind each counting other better than himself; 4 not looking each of you to his own things, but each of you also to the things of others.

In the genuine friendship of the Philippians, Paul felt a keen delight. With absolute sincerity he wrote, "I thank my God upon all my remembrance of you." There was, however, in the report brought by Epaphroditus one element which caused him real concern. He learned that a certain lack of harmony existed in the Philippian church. The discord could not have been very pronounced. The tone of the apostle's words are too tender for that. He does not rebuke. He does not warn. He only exhorts them all to "be of the same mind." The situation was very different from that at Corinth, where the church was divided into contending factions. Those Christians Paul found it necessary severely to admonish. He even threatened to come to them "with a rod."

The lack of Christian unity at Philippi was comparatively insignificant. It had only begun to develop. Yet it was real, and it is not at all difficult to imagine the causes which may have produced discord. It was a church composed of strongly contrasted elements. The beginning of its history would indicate that. The first converts included a wealthy purple dealer from Asia, a slave girl of Macedonia, a jailer in the service of Rome. These were examples of the diverse elements of which the church was composed. A group of persons so diverse in race, in culture, and in social standing might easily be divided into cliques and factions, particularly if there appeared among them individual men and women of masterful dispositions animated by something of ambition or pride.

Nor has there ever been a church in any age or place free from the peril of discord or immune to the danger of rivalry and strife. The exhortation of the apostle may be needed as much as ever by churches of the present day.

In the previous paragraph Paul has appealed to the Philippians to "stand fast in one spirit, with one soul striving for the faith of the gospel." Yet there the stress of the exhortation was upon the need of courage in the Christian "conflict." The emphasis was upon maintaining a right attitude toward common foes rather than a right relation toward fellow Christians. Here, with delicacy and yet with passionate earnestness, he pleads with them to nourish such a disposition as will produce unity of mind and heart and soul among the followers of Christ.

First of all he mentions the grounds on which his exhortation is based. He then sets forth the high character of that unity which he enjoins. Lastly he indicates those forces by which Christian unity may be destroyed and those by which it may be maintained.

He resumes the admonition to "stand fast in one spirit," as he says, "If there is therefore any exhortation in Christ." The "therefore" links the thought with that previous injunction. His meaning is this: "As I exhorted you to stand fast in one spirit, therefore complete my joy by being of one accord and one mind."

The "if" does not express uncertainty. It rather means "in view of the fact." It is intended to fix the thought successively on the various grounds of Paul's appeal. The first ground is that of the blessed experiences which the Philippians share in common as Christians: "If there exists," Paul is intimating, "any ground for exhortation based on your being in Christ." Surely an "exhortation in Christ" must be heeded. It is made in view of all that the Philippians have and are as followers of Christ.

The second ground of appeal is that of the tender persuasiveness of love. "If any consolation of love," writes Paul, meaning that, if love is any incentive to action, then they should heed Paul's exhortation. This seems to be the force of the word translated "comfort" in the King James Version. If "consolation" is the better translation, the meaning is not materially altered. The appeal is then based on all the encouragement and comfort which the readers have found in their mutual love or in the love of Christ.

The third ground is their "fellowship of the Spirit." As believers in Christ they have become partakers of the Holy Spirit. They have received from him new life and gifts and graces. It has been the operation of this one Spirit which has made them members of the church, the body of Christ. They should therefore seek to "keep the unity" which the Spirit gives "in the bond of peace."

The fourth ground for the appeal is found in those emotions which the Holy Spirit himself inspires, namely, "tender mercies and compassions." They have experienced and have manifested Christian affection and sympathy. Let such now be shown toward one another and toward himself. Let them now prove themselves to be tender-hearted and full of compassion and pity.

There is, however, another ground of appeal, although it is of the very substance of the exhortation: "Make full my joy," writes the apostle. If only he could see them standing fast "in one spirit, with one soul striving for the faith of the gospel," then indeed his cup of joy would be full. There is nothing selfish in basing his plea on his personal happiness. His friends will understand that his joy is ever found in their welfare. It is like the joy of a parent in the well-being of a child. Thus his readers know that only their highest good can give gladness to Paul. Something of the joy he feels in his relationship with them he has expressed in earlier passages of the epistle. Such joy may now be complete. Paul declares that it will be perfect if they manifest among themselves that unity for which he here pleads.

The unity is defined in general by the phrase, "That ye be of the same mind," and then more specifically by the phrases which follow. "Having the same love" indicates "the cherishing of mutual affection." "Being of one accord, of one mind" has been translated with even more fulness of expression, "With harmony of feeling giving your minds to one and the same object."

It is evident, then, that the Christian unity for which Paul pleads is something far deeper than assent to a common creed, or union in a form of worship, or fellowship in a common task. It underlies all these. It is a unity of heart as well as of mind. It is a unity of sentiment and of mutual love.

Perhaps it should be noticed here that this high ideal of Christian unity may not always be possible of attainment. In any church there may exist members so disagreeable and contentious that peace and harmony cannot be attained. Such a situation did not exist at Philippi. Paul felt that, as is usual, any discord which had arisen or might arise there could be removed by applying the motives to which he had appealed. In more serious cases more drastic measures, on occasion, must be employed.

Again it may be noted that among thoughtful people there cannot always be unanimity of opinion or belief. It can hardly be expected where there is independence of thought and freedom of expression that all will be "of the same mind." However, where there is "the same love," there will be broad tolerance and mutual consideration. There may be an agreement to disagree. Even if it seems wiser to separate for worship or for work, there can be unison in aim and purpose, and those who differ in their views can be heard "speaking truth in love."

Such disagreements or separations had not occurred among the Philippians Paul believed that, as in the case of most Christian churches, every necessity could be met, and perfect concord could be maintained, by a fuller emphasis upon such principles of action as almost inevitably animate those who remember that they are one "in Christ," and who realize the "fellowship of the Spirit."

Paul now indicates to his readers how this unity may be broken and how it may be maintained. He warns them against "faction" and "vainglory." He urges upon them humility and unselfishness.

"Faction" is a partisan spirit which engenders strife. Paul already has written that in Rome he is seeing its horrid results. (Ch. 1:17.) He is anxious that it shall not be allowed to distress his beloved church at Philippi. "Vainglory" denotes boastful pride. It is the spirit which inclines one to make great claims for himself and to disparage others. Literally it indicates emptiness of ideas.

Very often it is the empty-headed man who is loudest in his expressions of vanity and conceit. It is noticeable that religious zeal often breeds a spirit of "faction" and "vainglory."

It is indeed the spirit, quite as truly as any specific action, that Paul here deprecates. The phrase, "Doing nothing through faction or through vainglory," might quite as properly be rendered, "Thinking nothing by way of pride in vainglory"; for Paul has just been urging unity of thought, and he now commends "lowliness of mind." Ambition and vanity can destroy the harmony of any church, but concord will ever be maintained in any church or company which is characterized by "lowliness of mind."

This last phrase is elsewhere translated by the word "humility." The Greek word seems to be a creation of Christian writers. At least it has not appeared in existing compositions which are older than the New Testament. In classical Greek the adjective from which it is derived denoted "abjectness," "meanness," "baseness." The term in its Christian usage describes a spiritual grace or virtue, and possibly the highest of all the virtues. It is the very opposite of pride and self-glory. In indicates not merely modesty but self-forgetfulness, or such a lowly view of self as enables one to form rightful views of others, to take an interest in the welfare of others, to lose self in the service of others.

Thus, as indicated here, it enables each person to count others "better than himself." This Christian ideal is surprising; by some it is regarded as unreasonable. It is asserted that proper self-respect could not admit such an estimate of others. It is argued that we may have conclusive proof that others are less worthy and less able than ourselves. However, is it safe for us to act on such a judgment? We know our own weakness and defects; if we are lowly-minded these will be painfully obvious. Do we know the motives and temptations, the latent possibilities and actual capacities of others? Usually it is unwise to proceed on the assumption of our own superiority and our greater importance. Nor is the phrase to be pressed too far. The obvious intention of the apostle is to enjoin upon Christians real humility and unselfishness. Where these kindred virtues prevail, Christian unity is ever maintained, and believers are certain to be "of one accord, of one mind."

C. TO THE IMITATION OF CHRIST
Ch. 2:5-11

5 Have this mind in you, which was also in Christ Jesus: 6 who, existing in the form of God, counted not the being on an equality with God a thing to be grasped, 7 but emptied himself, taking the form of a servant, being made in the likeness of men; 8 and being found in fashion as a man, he humbled himself, becoming obedient even unto death, yea, the death of the cross. 9 Wherefore also God highly exalted him, and gave unto him the name which is above every name; 10 that in the name of Jesus every knee should bow, of things in heaven and things on earth and things under the earth, 11 and that every tongue should confess that Jesus Christ is Lord, to the glory of God the Father.

The most important events can be traced quite commonly to comparatively insignificant causes. Thus a slight discord in an obscure church, possibly a misunderstanding between two women, became the occasion of what is possibly the most significant statement ever made by Paul in relation to the incarnation and death and exaltation of Christ; and upon this statement he bases his most inspiring appeal to imitate Christ. For the true imitation of Christ does not consist merely in trying to imagine and to do the things which Christ would do, but in seeking to cultivate the spirit and the disposition which Christ revealed.

"Have this mind in you, which was also in Christ Jesus," writes the apostle. By the "mind" of Christ is meant his moral temper, his way of thinking, and specifically his humble and unselfish devotion. Some modern scholars would give a different interpretation to these words: "Have this mind in your community," or "Treat one another" in accordance with your "thought of Christ," or your "experience in Christ." The Greek is difficult. However, the more familiar translation seems to be supported by the connection. Paul wishes his readers to cherish a mental attitude, not simply in accordance with their own Christian thinking and experience, but conformed to the mind of Christ. Thus properly the phrase introduces the statement which follows, in which the example of Christ is set forth.

He regarded no sacrifice as too great, no humiliation as too painful, in accomplishing his redeeming work. It is this example, this way of thinking, this divine disposition, which Paul would have his readers reproduce. Such humility, such devotion to the interests of others could not fail to secure in this church at Philippi the unity for which Paul pleads.

This mind of Christ, therefore, does not refer to the mental activity or the intellectual processes of the man Jesus Christ. It describes the disposition of the eternal Son of God, even before he entered upon his earthly career, indeed the very humility and devotion which led him to accept that career with its pain and misery and death. It is the "mind" of that divine Savior, "who, existing in the form of God, counted not the being on an equality with God a thing to be grasped."

Every phrase of this verse and of those which immediately follow has been the subject of extended controversy. It is helpful to remember that Paul is not attempting to establish subtle theological dogmas, nor to explain profound mysteries. He is simply stating accepted facts in order to enforce obvious duty. He is only saying that as Christ stooped from heaven to earth that he might secure our redemption, so his followers should be willing to make sacrifices and to undertake lowly, self-forgetful tasks in the service of others. Paul is thus using the voluntary humiliation of Christ as an example of that unselfish devotion by which the unity of the church can be maintained.

It may be remarked, however, that Paul's witness to the eternal existence, to the divine nature, and to the incarnation of Christ is all the more important because he mentions them thus incidentally, and as matters of fact universally accepted to which he could refer to secure a practical result.

In this reference to the existence of Christ before he became man, Paul states that he was "in the form of God." When used in such a connection the word "form" cannot denote a physical shape, much less a merely apparent likeness. It signifies rather the nature of God, his character, the very essence of his being. Paul means to affirm, not merely that Christ was like God, but that he was God. He does not ascribe to him the divinity which in some sense men may claim as the created "offspring" of God, but actual and essential deity.

Not only was Christ "in the form of God," but he was also "on an equality with God." The latter phrase refers not to nature but to relation. He was the eternal Son of God and as such he shared the glory of the Father. His divine nature he could never lay aside; his glory, however, he might relinquish. He ever would be essential deity; but he might assume a humbler mode of being. Thus, he "counted not the being on an equality with God a thing to be grasped, but emptied himself." The phrase, "A thing to be grasped," probably means, not "a thing to be taken possession of by violence," but "a thing to be laid hold of and retained." Christ did not so regard his eternal glory; but he divested himself of that glory. This is apparently the meaning of the phrase translated "Emptied himself."

Many other theories have been advocated to define or explain this "emptying," or kenosis (Greek, $\kappa\acute{\epsilon}\nu\omega\sigma\iota\varsigma$). The attempt is made to show what divine attributes Christ gave up in order to become man. The endeavor is to explain the relation between the divine and the human nature of Christ. These theories are not without interest, possibly not without real profit. One must ever be careful to maintain, however, that Christ did not and could not cease to be divine, but that he could and he did lay aside "the insignia of his majesty," the outward manifestations of his deity. All that this meant for Christ one cannot faintly imagine. Paul does not seek to penetrate into the mystery. That it involved an infinite sacrifice is the truth he seeks to impress.

It is best, however, to turn from mere conjecture to the definite statements of the apostle. According to his words, "emptying" on the part of Christ consisted in his "taking the form of a servant," and "being made in the likeness of men." The first phrase is in striking contrast with "existing in the form of God." That significant word "form" thus appears again. As Christ existed from eternity in the "form of God," so now, in time, he takes on himself the form of man. As he shared the very nature and attributes of God, so now he has the true nature and attributes of a servant. However, in assuming the "form of a servant," he does not lose the "form of God." He lays aside his divine glory but not his divine nature. However, his manner of existence is now that of a "servant," a "slave." The same divine Being who, with the Father, had been supreme over all now becomes servant of all, and wholly submissive to his Father's will.

The second phrase, "Being made in the likeness of men," describes the true manhood assumed by Christ. However, Paul does not use here the term "form," but "likeness." Christ was really man, but not merely man. His likeness to men was actual yet this did not constitute his entire self. His humanity was real yet his being was still divine. The very word "likeness" asserts similarity but denies identity. Those who find in Christ only ideal manhood and nothing more have not yet discovered the Christ of Paul and the Christ of the universal church.

This Christ is at once God and man.

He was "found in fashion as a man." His outward appearance was altogether human. He so appeared to men. They so regarded him. He was so "found" by them. Such was his "fashion," his outward guise. In reality he was much more. Had the eyes of men been opened they would have realized that they who had seen him had seen the Father. Yet they saw in him only a man, and indeed a man who was "despised, and rejected, . . . a man of sorrows, and acquainted with grief"; for his voluntary humiliation did not consist merely in assuming actual humanity, but "he humbled himself, becoming obedient even unto death, yea, the death of the cross."

His voluntary humiliation which made him wholly subject to the will of his Father led him even as far as death, and that, too, death in its most terrible and revolting form. The cross was the very symbol of disgrace, agony, and shame. Crucifixion could be inflicted upon no Roman citizen. It was visited only upon the worst of criminals. To one who suffered this mode of death the law of Moses attached a curse. (Deut. 21:23; Gal. 3:13.) With the mention of such ignominy the picture of Christ's stooping from glory reaches its climax. His unselfish service brought him all the way from the throne of divine majesty to the cross on Calvary.

Such a vision is enough to consume all "faction" and "vainglory," and to "pour contempt" on all our pride. Such an example should make us think less of our own interests and more of the interests of others, and forget self in loving service.

The further incentive to such unselfish devotion is given in the description which follows of the exaltation of Christ. We find in him an illustration of his own teaching. "He that humbleth himself shall be exalted." The way of the cross is after all the way of light, and the path which leads to abiding power. One should not serve and suffer in the selfish hope of thereby securing advancement and personal gain; yet one who endures in obedient submission to God and with devoted love for others will find that there await him, in time or in eternity, a scepter and a throne.

"Wherefore also," because of his humility and devotion, "God highly exalted him." Not only did he raise him from the dead but he gave back to him all that he had renounced. He granted him all power "in heaven and on earth." He welcomed him to the glory which he had shared with him before the world began. As Paul states in his epistle to the Ephesians, God "made him to sit at his right hand in the heavenly places, far above all rule, and authority, and power, and dominion, and every name that is named, not only in this world, but also in that which is to come."

This is what Paul means here, in writing to the Philippians, as he adds, "And gave unto him the name which is above every name." He is referring to the dignity, the glory, the redeeming power, the divine supremacy, granted to Christ as the consequence of his atoning work and as the natural expression of his divine nature.

A name is that by which one is known. An ideal "name" is that which one is known to be. It describes one's character, position, place, and nature. This is a familar use of the term in both the Old Testament and the New. "His name shall be called Wonderful, Counsellor, Mighty God, Everlasting Father, Prince of Peace." These were not to be the actual titles of the coming Messiah; but he was to be all that those titles indicated. So when Christ said to his disciples, "Whatsoever ye shall ask in my name, that will I do," and when he bade them henceforth always to pray in his "name," he meant that they were to pray in virtue of all that he was and was to be, with faith in all he had done for them and would do, with submission to him and complete dependence upon him as their Master and Savior and Lord.

Thus the "name which is above every name" does not mean the word "Jesus" or the word "Lord." Our Savior was given the name "Jesus" and he was known as "Lord" during the days of his humiliation. Neither name was given to him when he was exalted to the right hand of God. The "name of Jesus" does not mean any word, any title, any appellation, but it denotes all that Jesus is now known to be, as Son of God and Son of Man, as the divine Savior and Redeemer. It is "in the name of Jesus," in virtue and in recognition of all that he is and of all that he has done, that every knee shall bow to him and every tongue shall confess that he is "Lord."

It is not "at the name of Jesus," but "in the name of Jesus" that homage is to be rendered. Paul does not mean that worshipers should bow at the mention of the word "Jesus," but that in virtue of his saving work and his divine power every knee should bow before him in worship and in prayer and every tongue should be vocal in confession and in praise.

This recognition is to be rendered by all, whether "in heaven" or "on earth" or "under the earth." These phrases are not to be pressed too far, as though they designated specifically angels, men, and demons, or celestial beings, those who dwell on earth, and the dead in the underworld or in the place of departed spirits. The description is general, and points to the universal acknowledgment of the grace and glory and sovereignty of Christ.

Such worship of the Son is not displeasing to the Father. It is in Christ that God is revealed. Men are granted "the light of the knowledge of the glory of God in the face of Jesus Christ." The adoration of Christ and submission to him as Lord is not idolatry, for he is not a creature but is himself divine. All honor paid to Christ is, as Paul here concludes, "to the glory of God the Father."

D. TO EARNEST ENDEAVOR Ch. 2:12-18

12 So then, my beloved, even as ye have always obeyed, not as in my presence only, but now much more in my ab-

sence, work out your own salvation with fear and trem-
bling;   13 for it is God who worketh in you both to will
and to work, for his good pleasure.   14 Do all things with-
out murmurings and questionings: 15 that ye may become
blameless and harmless, children of God without blemish
in the midst of a crooked and perverse generation, among
whom ye are seen as lights in the world, 16 holding forth
the word of life; that I may have whereof to glory in the
day of Christ, that I did not run in vain neither labor in
vain.   17 Yea, and if I am offered upon the sacrifice and
service of your faith, I joy, and rejoice with you all: 18
and in the same manner do ye also joy, and rejoice with
me.

Paul is always intensely practical. He ever relates doctrine and duty, creed and character, faith and life. He
never makes the mistake of supposing that religion consists in assent to certain dogmas, nor does he fall into that
more common error of imagining that morality can be
maintained without religious faith.

Thus when exhorting his readers to that humble and
self-forgetting devotion by which unity can be preserved,
he gave them the inspiring example of Christ, who for
their sakes exchanged the glories of heaven for earthly
suffering, even for the cruel cross. Yet this humiliation
resulted in his being given the place of supreme dignity
and power. Thus this same example of obedience to the
will of God, and its blessed issue, is used by the apostle
as a basis for his further exhortation to fulfill the will of
God by earnest endeavor for spiritual progress and by
consistent witness as followers of Christ.

"So then, my beloved," writes the apostle, as though
he were saying, "In view of the obedience of Christ and its
divine reward, show that same obedience which you have
always manifested," and, "Not as in my presence only,
but now much more in my absence, work out your own
salvation with fear and trembling." It would be a higher
manifestation of loyalty and devotion to be absolutely

faithful when Paul was away from them in Rome than to be faithful when they were still enjoying the stimulating help of his personal presence. None are so worthy of praise as those whose obedience to the will of God is quite independent of the knowledge and admiration of men.

However, whether in his presence or absence, these Christians are urged to "work out" their "own salvation." It is after all their "own." Their effort must not depend upon him, and its issue chiefly concerns themselves. Paul does not say that they are to "work for" their own salvation, as though it were something to be received as a reward of merit or even as a result of effort. They are to work it "out," as something already enjoyed, possessed in principle or in part.

"Salvation" is a large and inclusive term. It is found in the New Testament with various shades of meaning. It sometimes expresses the whole experience of a believer from the time he accepts Christ as a Savior until he is made perfect in glory. At other times it may indicate any one of the three phases of that experience. It may denote deliverance from the guilt of sin, or deliverance from the power of sin, or final deliverance from the presence and the result of sin. Paul in his epistles gives illustrations of all these uses of the word. Here the meaning is related to the second of these. Paul is addressing believers who have already accepted Christ, who have found pardon and new life through faith in him. He is writing to those who, in this sense, already have been saved. He is urging them, however, to carry their salvation to completion. There are victories to be won. There are virtues to be developed. There are crowns to be obtained.

In their earnest endeavor, these Christians are to strive "with fear and trembling." The words do not denote slavish or cowardly terror, but submission and reverence toward God, and a humble distrust of self. There is something too jaunty and self-confident and flippant in the attitude of many Christians toward their "own salvation."

It is necessary to watch and pray, to strive, and to work. One must labor earnestly and with a lowly dread of displeasing God. One must feel a "trembling" anxiety to do his holy will. One must be conscious of his own weakness and continual moral peril.

Such effort is not inconsistent with faith. It is, indeed, the truest expression of trust. A faith which does not express itself in such reverent and earnest effort is false and dead. Nor does Paul see the least contradiction between urging believers to work out their own salvation and assuring them that God is working in them. The very fact that God is working is given as the ground of the exhortation for them to work.

Here thus are stated the two great realities of divine sovereignty and human free agency. The work is the work of God, and at the same time it is the work of man. God does not do one part of the work and man another part. The whole work is of God and the whole work is of man. Paul does not attempt to reconcile the apparent conflict of thought. The very command to "work" implies freedom and responsibility and duty. On the other hand, the divine operation is described as continuous and ultimate. God "worketh in you both to will and to work." That is, the impulses and desires which lead to action are ascribed to God. Nor does he simply provide the outward circumstances which result in emotions and choices. He exercises a direct, inner operation upon the spirit of man.

Nor does the working of God stop with motives and desires or even with the action of the will. All the outward acts and deeds of a Christian, as well as his thoughts and impulses, are attributed to God. "It is God who worketh in you," not only "to will," but also "to work." All the good in the heart and life of the believer is thus ascribed to the activity of God. Furthermore, it is "for his good pleasure." All that God does springs from his mercy and his love. It is carrying out his own gracious plan. His purpose is the salvation of believers. To accomplish his will he surrounds them with the influences of his Holy Spirit. As one seeks to work out his own salvation he is encouraged by the belief that at the same time, in every right resolve and action and deed, God is working in him.

The consciousness of human freedom and responsibility must not be allowed to weaken conviction in the unlimited activity and operation of God. All attempts to reconcile the apparent opposition between these two beliefs have failed. The endeavor to secure harmony has usually consisted in a partial denial or neglect of either one or the other of the truths involved. The reason for failure is due to our imperfect knowledge of God and of man.

The real peril lies, however, not in the sphere of speculation or reasoning, but in the sphere of practical experience. The sense of human responsibility leads to despair unless balanced by confidence in the grace and power of God. Belief in the power and activity of God, unless accompanied by human determination and conscious effort, results in moral impotence and disaster.

True confidence in God results in humble, active obedience. It enables one to "do all things without murmurings and questionings." One whose faith in God is weak soon falls before the temptations of questioning the will and providence of God and of finding grounds for contention with his neighbors. "Murmuring" was a continual and serious defect in the conduct of Israel during the wilderness journey; it too often is heard among the people of God today. Paul had "learned, in whatsoever state" he was, "therein to be content." He could "rejoice in the Lord" under all circumstances. Even in prison he could write this epistle of joy. His example is one that all should seek to follow.

"Questionings" refers to skeptical doubts and criticisms, which result in distrust of God and in rebellion against his will. These are too often expressed in open "disputes," as the word is also translated. Paul is here concerned with the conduct which results from such a frame of mind. He wishes to guard his readers against it. His desire is that they "may become blameless and harmless."

The word "become" implies a process of development. It is part of that "salvation" which they are to "work out." They are to become "blameless." They are to give the world no ground for criticism. Men are sure to find fault; but the conduct of Christians should be free from imperfection in the judgment of God as well as in the judgment of conscience and of their fellowmen. Such a high ideal Paul places before his readers.

Further, they are to be "harmless." This English word is somewhat weakened by modern use. The Greek implies that which is "unmixed," "unadulterated," or "unalloyed." Possibly "pure gold" is a popular designation of the moral quality implied. Christians are to avoid those inconsistencies at which the world can point a finger of scorn. Their lives are to be all of one piece, not part belonging to God and part to sin and self. Their robes are to be free from spot or stain. Their characters are to be transparent and sincere.

Their lives are to form a striking contrast with those of men of the world. They are to be "children of God without blemish in the midst of a crooked and perverse generation." "Children of God" is here to be interpreted in its usual New Testament sense. It refers to those who have experienced a new birth through faith in Christ. They have been "begotten of God," "born of God." They are partakers of his nature. As such they are to reveal themselves to men. They are to appear "without blemish," without "reproach," "faultless," in the midst of "a crooked and perverse generation."

The last phrase is quoted from Deut. 32:5, where ancient Israel is described as forgetful of the God who as a father had brought the nation into being and claimed it as his own firstborn son among the peoples of the world. Because of their forgetfulness and disobedience they had become "perverse and crooked." Here by way of contrast the true "children of God," the followers of Christ, are to fulfill their divine calling and purpose by lives which are to be so submissive to the will of God that they will be "blameless and harmless" and "without blemish" in a world which is "crooked," or indocile, rebellious, froward, and "perverse," or morally distorted.

Israel, by being "perverse and crooked," had failed to accomplish its mission of witnessing for God to the surrounding nations; the "children of God" were accomplishing their mission by consistent, obedient lives which made them to be "seen as lights in the world."

The word "lights" is really "luminaries." It refers, not to any earthly or human means of illumination, but to the stars and other heavenly bodies. As the moon and the planets and the constellations shine forth in brightness against the blackness of the night, so the lives of true Christians lighten the moral darkness of the world. They do so by "holding forth the word of life." The duty of Christians, therefore, is not merely to form a moral contrast to the godless world, but to bear witness to the Source from whence all true life issues. The gospel which they proclaim is in all reality "the word of life," for it contains the principle and power of the life which is life indeed, the life which is more abundant, the life which is "hid with Christ in God," the life which someday will be manifested in all its perfection and glory when Christ appears.

Christians must "hold forth" this glad message by public and worldwide proclamation, yet also by the silent witness of lives and characters which are "lights in the world." Indeed, the preaching of "the word" has little power unless it is attested by conduct which is "blameless and harmless" and "without blemish."

It was in order that such consistent Christian lives might shed their radiance in a dark world that Paul has endured hardship and suffering and toil as a messenger of Christ.

He is eager that those among whom he has labored may so live that he may be proud of them and may rejoice in them on the day when Christ returns. That day will be for the Christian worker the day of reward and recompense. Work will be reviewed and prizes given. Paul is unwilling to find that all his effort and sacrifice have been in vain. He would not have it then appear that he has been running for a phantom prize and enduring weariness for an imaginary reward, or, as he expresses his hope, "that I may have whereof to glory in the day of Christ, that I did not run in vain neither labor in vain." Thus Paul relates his very joy in heaven to the fidelity and consistent living of those for whom he labors while on earth.

This desire for satisfaction and glory "in the day of Christ" is in no sense selfish. If Paul's followers will continue by their unblemished character to hold "forth the word of life," he is willing to die for them. "Yea, and if I am offered upon the sacrifice and service of your faith," he writes, "I joy, and rejoice with you all."

The "faith" of the Philippians meant, not only their acceptance of Christ and their trust in him, but all the deeds and the devotion by which their faith was expressed. It is pictured in phrases borrowed from the ritual of the ancient sacrifices. The words, "I am offered," are literally, "I am poured out as a drink-offering." The term "service" indicates a "priestly ministration." Thus the meaning of Paul's words may be more fully expressed, "If my blood is poured out as a libation upon the sacrifice and the priestly service which consists in your faith, I joy, and rejoice with you all."

Paul was face to face with death. A man on trial for his life at the judgment seat of Nero was threatened by no imaginary danger. One cannot fail, then, to note the courage of the old hero. He was absolutely unafraid. He could allude to all the impending horrors of a Roman execution as merely the offering of a libation to God. He held no morbid view of life. He indulged in no sickly

sentiment as to death. He was willing either to die or
to live.

Paul has been urging upon his readers humility and
obedience to God and submission to the divine will. Here
he furnishes in his own case an admirable example. He
has "the mind of Christ," the "mind" he is urging upon
his readers. He is ready for service or sacrifice, which-
ever may lie in the way of God's choosing.

It should be noticed, too, how his attitude toward imminent death is related to the possibility of service. In
the first chapter he suppresses his "desire to depart and
be with Christ" because he feels that his continuing with
them is necessary for the Philippians' "progress and joy
in the faith." Here he expresses his joy at the prospect of
death in case this may strengthen and perfect and complete "the sacrifice and service of . . . [their] faith."

"I joy," he writes, referring to his possible execution,
"and rejoice with you all," referring to the gladness they
are finding in their new life of Christian experience and
service.

"In the same manner," continues the apostle, "do ye
also joy, and rejoice with me," that is, in the very prospect
of his suffering death in the service of Christ. It is not
often that men regard martyrdom as a ground for con-
gratulation. However, if life is an offering and a priestly
service to God, and if death is a libation poured out in
his worship, then it may be possible in view of either event
to "joy, and rejoice."

IV
PAUL'S COMPANIONS
IN ROME
Ch. 2:19-30

A. THE MISSION OF TIMOTHY   Ch. 2:19-24

*19 But I hope in the Lord Jesus to send Timothy shortly
unto you, that I also may be of good comfort, when I know
your state.   20 For I have no man likeminded, who will
care truly for your state.   21 For they all seek their own,
not the things of Jesus Christ.   22 But ye know the proof
of him, that, as a child serveth a father, so he served with
me in furtherance of the gospel.   23 Him therefore I hope
to send forthwith, so soon as I shall see how it will go with
me: 24 but I trust in the Lord that I myself also shall
come shortly.*

The epistle to the Philippians is informal.   It is not,
however, without order.   A general sequence of thought
can be observed.   Paul begins by informing his readers as
to his own experiences and adding certain practical exhortations.   Not unnaturally he then mentions the plans of
the two friends who have been serving and cheering him
during his confinement in Rome.   These are Timothy and
Epaphroditus.   Their names may be linked quite logically
with the exhortations which precede.   Paul has been urging upon the Philippians the necessity of self-forgetful,
humble service.   The supreme example given has been
that of Christ.   However, Paul has expressed his own willingness to die in the service of his friends; and now he
mentions two companions whose lives have been devoted
to loving ministries and sympathetic care.
The connection of thought seems to be more immediate

still. Paul has mentioned his martyrdom, not only as a possibility but as a ground for rejoicing, if it is to strengthen the faith of the Philippians and is to crown his labors for them. However, he instinctively realizes that this mention of his death will cast a shadow over the hearts of his readers. This shadow he will at once dispel. He does so by expressing his confident hope and expectation that he is to be acquitted and set free. As soon as this favorable judgment is pronounced, Paul is to send Timothy to Philippi with the good news and is to receive from the Philippians tidings of their welfare.

"But I hope in the Lord Jesus," writes Paul, "to send Timothy shortly unto you, that I also may be of good comfort, when I know your state." His "hope" is "in the Lord Jesus," for all Paul's plans and purposes center in Christ. He lives in Christ. He can truthfully say, "To me to live is Christ." Thus this hope of sending Timothy is to be fulfilled only if Christ permits; and if it is fulfilled, then the mission of Timothy is to be in the service of Christ, and for the sake of Christ.

The message of Timothy is to be of Paul's release. With charming delicacy and modesty Paul indicates this supremely important substance of the message only by the little word "also," as he says, "That I also may be of good comfort." This evidently indicates that the news from Paul will bring "good comfort" to the Philippians. It must then be tidings of Paul's acquittal. However, Paul implies that his main purpose in sending Timothy is that he may receive tidings of his friends in Philippi, as though their condition is of more importance than the continued life of the apostle. Still further does Paul imply that news from Philippi will be good news: "That I also may be of good comfort, when I know your state." Thus does Paul express his sense of the importance of the Philippian church, and his confidence in its spiritual well-being and loyalty to Christ.

There will be, however, a further purpose in this mission

of Timothy. He is to encourage and guide and help the Philippians. In the continued absence of Paul, he is to supply for them all those spiritual blessings which Paul himself might have brought. There is, however, a deep pathos in the way Paul states this purpose: "For I have no man likeminded, who will care truly for your state." There is no other messenger whom Paul can send who is competent and willing to render this service.

Undoubtedly there were many persons in Rome willing to go on such a mission but they were not able to go. Others there were who were able to go but not qualified to go. However, of those who were free to go and competent for the service, Timothy was the only one who was willing to undertake the task. He was the only one who would take a genuine interest in the Philippians. He was the only one who would "care truly" for their spiritual welfare. No other man was "likeminded."

The reason why there were no others ready to volunteer for this mission is stated by the apostle in his regretful words, "For they all seek their own, not the things of Jesus Christ." This is a startling statement. It cannot be denied that it comes to the reader with a certain sad surprise. Nor is it strange that it has been the occasion of much speculation and controversy. Paul has even been accused of despondency and of exaggeration and of other faults hardly in harmony with the uniform character of this hymn of joy and calm friendliness.

However, the question is inevitable: Where were the other friends of Paul's imprisonment? Where were Luke and Aristarchus and Tychicus and Onesimus and Epaphras and John Mark? Surely Paul intended to bring no charge of selfishness against these loved comrades. We have only fragments of the story. Probably these companions had not yet reached the city or had been sent on some of those many missions which were involved in Paul's "care of all the churches," particularly during the days of his confinement in Rome.

What is more significant is the fact that there are few, pitifully few, messengers whom the Master can send forth today on missions and ministries of love at home and abroad. For some of these forms of service not many are qualified, but of others the words of Paul are pathetically true: "They all seek their own, not the things of Jesus Christ."

To such Timothy forms a striking contrast. Of this the Philippians are well aware: "But ye know the proof of him." The word "proof" indicates not only that which is revealed by testing but also that which results from testing. The Philippians are fully acquainted with his approved worth, his sterling character. They have learned by experience his loyalty and love. They remember how severely at Philippi he had been tried and how nobly he had survived the ordeal.

His character, however, has been especially revealed in his devoted service and support of Paul. It is like the service of a son to a revered parent: "As a child serveth a father." Paul is about to add, "So he served me." This would have been true. However, he interrupts himself. With extreme humility and loving deference he says, "He served with me." He raises Timothy to the position of an equal, a fellow laborer, a fellow messenger. This united service was "in furtherance of the gospel."

It is in such slight touches that the nobility and sensitiveness of the character of Paul appears. One can well understand why he had faithful friends, and why one like Timothy was so devoted to his great leader, and so ready to undertake any mission which Paul might propose. It is true that no friendships in the world are so close and inspiring as those in which lives are united in loyal service of Christ, seeking for the "furtherance of the gospel."

This trusted messenger Paul expects to send "shortly." He will wait, however, until he learns the issue of his own trial. That issue is still uncertain. Who can predict the verdict of a Nero? How can one anticipate the caprice

of a tyrant?   Whether acquittal or execution await him
Paul cannot tell.   The decision, however, may not be long
delayed, and Timothy will hasten to Philippi with the fate-
ful news.   "Him therefore I hope to send forthwith, so
soon as I shall see how it will go with me."   Thus calmly
does Paul await the decision.   Thus fearlessly does he look
into the unknown future.   Busy with his task, interested
in the welfare of his fellow Christians, he awaits the voice
which he will recognize as the voice of God, the voice
which will announce for him either deliverance or death.

However, he waits in an attitude of hope.   He has no
weak longing to die, no cowardly desire to escape from the
ills of life.   He recognizes the fact that his continued activity may mean much of blessing to others.   For their
sake he wishes to live.   With confidence in Christ, and
with a recognition of the importance of his service, he
believes that he not only can soon send the joyful news of
his acquittal, but can come in person to bring comfort and
gladness to the hearts of his friends: "But I trust in the
Lord that I myself also shall come shortly."   His hope and
his confidence are "in the Lord."   If release comes, it will
be only by the grace and power of the Lord.   If this hope
is not fulfilled, something even better will result.   If Paul
cannot visit Philippi, he will start upon a more triumphant
journey to a land where there are no shadows.   In either
case the will of the Lord will be done.   Paul is well
content.

B. THE RETURN OF EPAPHRODITUS
Ch. 2:25-30

*25 But I counted it necessary to send to you Epaphro-
ditus, my brother and fellow-worker and fellow-soldier,
and your messenger and minister to my need; 26 since he
longed after you all, and was sore troubled, because ye had
heard that he was sick: 27 for indeed he was sick nigh
unto death: but God had mercy on him; and not on him
only, but on me also, that I might not have sorrow upon*

sorrow. 28 I have sent him therefore the more diligently, that, when ye see him again, ye may rejoice, and that I may be the less sorrowful. 29 Receive him therefore in the Lord with all joy; and hold such in honor: 30 because for the work of Christ he came nigh unto death, hazarding his life to supply that which was lacking in your service toward me.

Paul had a second companion whose presence cheered the long hours of his imprisonment in Rome. This was Epaphroditus, a member, possibly an officer, of the Philippian church. He was a man "likeminded" with Timothy and with Paul himself. He had "the mind of Christ," the spirit of humble and self-sacrificing service. To him had been assigned the duty of bringing to Rome the bounty of Paul's friends in Philippi. On his arrival he proved to be an invaluable help to the apostle. He comforted him by his companionship, he assisted him in preaching, he ministered to his bodily wants. However, he was seized with a violent illness which nearly proved fatal. News of this illness, but not of his recovery, reached Philippi; subsequently word of the extreme anxiety of his friends was brought to him in Rome.

As a result, Epaphroditus has become genuinely homesick and is weighed down with longing to see his loved companions and to relieve them of the distress which they are suffering on his account. Paul would have retained him gladly, but in utter unselfishness he now sends him back to Philippi, bearing this letter in which he expresses his gratitude for the gift which the church has sent and also his deep and tender appreciation of all that Epaphroditus has been to him and has done for him.

"But I counted it necessary to send to you Epaphroditus," he writes. Timothy is coming soon, Paul expects to follow, but there will be uncertainty and delay. The anxiety of the Philippians must be relieved. They are in need of admonition and encouragement. Paul wishes to learn of their welfare. Epaphroditus is heavy-hearted and

distressed. Paul regards it as absolutely "necessary" to
send him back to Philippi. He does not blame him for
wishing to return. In fact the references to him in this
paragraph form a glowing and affectionate eulogy. They
are even more: they constitute a biography. They embody
all that is known of this Philippian Christian, but they give
to his character reality and life, and they surround his
name with a halo of unfading glory. Yet, much more than
this, they afford another glimpse into the heart of the
apostle, and reveal his nobleness, his courtesy, his tenderness, his unselfish love.

He generously places his servant and assistant on an
equality with himself. He calls him his "brother" in the
faith, his "fellow-worker" in proclaiming the gospel, his
"fellow-soldier" in the conflict with the enemies of Christ.
Thus he makes him one with himself in sympathy, in service, and in suffering. He also describes him as the "messenger" of the Philippians, using the word "apostle,"
which, while correctly rendered "messenger," may have
something of the dignity of the term commonly associated
with Paul and other official witnesses for Christ. Thus
Epaphroditus is the appointed and honored representative
of the Philippian church. He is also called their "minister" to Paul's need. The word describes one who is engaged in a "priestly service," just as later in the epistle
Paul designates the gift brought by Epaphroditus as a
"sacrifice," an "oblation" to God. Thus does Paul, with
true spiritual insight, express the real dignity of all tasks
undertaken in the name of Christ and in his service. Epaphroditus was probably engaged chiefly in humble or
menial tasks in providing for the physical needs of the
apostle. Yet his honor is as great as that of Paul, and he
is acting as the official representative and priestly servant
of the entire church at Philippi.

The immediate occasion for the return of Epaphroditus
is the fact that he is pitifully homesick. "He longed after
you all," Paul explains; he "was sore troubled." This

longing to see his friends is not only due to his loneliness, and his experiences in Rome, but has been greatly aggravated by the news which has reached him of the deep anxiety felt for him in Philippi; as Paul states it, "Because ye had heard that he was sick." Just how this news had come to Epaphroditus is not certain—probably by a letter to which this epistle to the Philippians is in part a direct reply. Such messages from home, telling a man how truly he is loved and how solicitous others are for his welfare, may be gladly received, but they usually add to his longing to return to those from whom the message has come.

Homesickness was not limited to the apostolic age. There are those serving on distant fields today whose loneliness and anguish of heart are not dispelled even by the companionship of a Paul. It is part of the price one may pay for the privilege of being a "messenger and minister" of Christ.

The physical illness of Epaphroditus, which possibly was one cause for his sickness of heart, had been critical in the extreme. "Indeed he was sick nigh unto death," writes Paul. What caused this illness can only be conjectured. Possibly the long journey from Macedonia, or the living conditions in Rome, or overexertion in his service of Paul may have weakened the messenger from Philippi and made his body a prey to disease. In any event, his desperate suffering was a cause of boundless distress and deepest concern to Paul. His recovery was regarded by the apostle as an interposition of divine providence and a special manifestation of grace. "God had mercy on him," Paul writes, and then adds, "And not on him only, but on me also, that I might not have sorrow upon sorrow." The death of such a companion, if added to all the distress of Paul's imprisonment, would have been almost more than he could stand. It would have been a crushing blow when billow after billow of sorrow had already broken upon him, and he might have been overwhelmed. Such was Paul's affection, and such his love. They emphasize his unselfishness in sending away one so dear to his heart, one of whose companionship he was so much in need.

Paul's utter disregard of self appears further in the words which follow, which at first might seem to indicate that Paul was happy to send Epaphroditus. The fact is that Paul would gladly have kept him in Rome, but his joy lay in the happiness which was to come to Epaphroditus and to his friends in Philippi. Thus Paul declares, "I have sent him therefore the more diligently, that, when ye see him again, ye may rejoice, and that I may be the less sorrowful." So fully does Paul sympathize with Epaphroditus in his longing for home, so fully does he realize the anxiety of the Philippians, that the departure of Epaphroditus, which causes Paul the deepest regret, is said to afford him relief. He is made "less sorrowful"; a burden is lifted from his heart. It is the expectation of their joy which makes him glad. There is a certain sublimity of unselfishness in the case of one who finds relief in a personal loss by which others are to gain.

"I have sent him," writes Paul. The tense of the verb, and of the previous verb, "I counted it necessary to send . . . Epaphroditus," conform to a Greek idiom used in writing letters. Possibly they may be understood better if translated, "I am sending him," and "I count it necessary to send Epaphroditus." The recovery of Epaphroditus, his longing for Philippi, and the yearning of his friends have led Paul to make the sacrifice and to send Epaphroditus as the bearer of this epistle.

Such evident devotion of the Philippians to Epaphroditus and his manifest love for them seem to make Paul's closing exhortation unnecessary: "Receive him therefore in the Lord with all joy; and hold such in honor." Indeed some so misunderstand these words as to suppose that there was some unknown estrangement between Epaphroditus and the Philippians, which Paul seeks to remove. So to interpret these words, however, is to be blind to all the circumstances and forgetful of all that Paul has just said.

He knows the love of the Philippians for their trusted messenger and his love for them. Because of this mutual love he feels that the separation should end, and for this reason he is sending Epaphroditus home. It is this knowledge of their love that explains Paul's command. "In view of such love," so Paul seems to say, "no reception could be too royal, no welcome too cordial. Receive him as one whom the Lord is restoring to you. Welcome him as your brother in Christ, and show him the honor that is his just due."

The reason for such a reception and for such respect is further defined: "Because for the work of Christ he came nigh unto death, hazarding his life." The phrase, "Hazarding his life," might be rendered, "Putting his life at stake." It is a term borrowed from gambling, where a player assumes a great risk for a possible gain. So almost recklessly Epaphroditus had staked his life in the service of Christ.

The exact form of this service is described by Paul with inimitable graciousness. Epaphroditus is said to have endangered "his life to supply that which was lacking in your service toward me." Paul does not intimate that the Philippians had failed in their service and that Epaphroditus had done what they had neglected to do. Far otherwise is his meaning. He pays the most courteous tribute both to the Philippians and to Epaphroditus. He expresses his gratitude to both. He means that the gift had come from the whole church and that all that was lacking to make it perfect was the presence of his friends in Philippi. As this was impossible Epaphroditus had undertaken to present the gift, even at the peril of his own life. The service is described as a "priestly ministration." The gift of the Philippians was not only an offering to Paul but also a sacrifice to God well pleasing to him. Thus Paul compliments the Philippians upon their generosity and commends Epaphroditus for his unselfish devotion.

What reception did Epaphroditus receive in Philippi?

Is it necessary to inquire? Many faithful servants of Christ, however, are not given the recognition they deserve at the hands of the church. Their Master ultimately rewards them. As for Epaphroditus it may be affirmed that for his lowly service to Paul in his imprisonment he has been placed among the immortals. These words of praise, penned for him by his loyal friend, will be read when men have forgotten even the names of those Roman warriors who once fought for the empire of the world before the walls of the city where this humble follower of Christ had his home.

V
WARNINGS
Ch. 3

A. AGAINST LEGALISM   Ch. 3:1-16

Paul's praise of his friends is followed by a solemn rebuke of his foes. He has just commended Timothy and Epaphroditus to the Philippians; he now warns the Philippians against certain enemies of the church. Some people connect this warning and this praise most closely. They conjecture that the enemies of whom Paul speaks were in Rome, that they had bitterly attacked Epaphroditus, and that the mention of his name had led Paul to warn his readers against similar enemies in Philippi. This is hazarding a mere guess, as also is the theory that some other incident interrupted Paul in his writing and induced him to give these warnings when he resumed his work. Any such supposition may be right or it may be wrong. It is wholly imaginary. Nor is it necessary. This friendly letter is quite informal. Paul passes easily from one subject to another. To some the change of thought here seems so abrupt as to demand the explanation of a sudden episode in the experience of the writer. The more common view is that the order of thought is quite natural. Paul has been writing of the return of Epaphroditus to Philippi, and of a coming visit from Timothy and even from Paul himself. This letter is to close shortly with thanks to the Philippians. It is not at all surprising that as he is thinking so intently of these friends he includes in his practical and informal message some mention of the serious perils concerning which he had often spoken. These perils were not so much those which concerned him in Rome as those which threatened the church at Philippi.

They were due to two classes of persons. One of these professed faith in Christ but wished to bind upon the church the laws of Moses. Those belonging to the other class, under the guise of Christian liberty, were living in pagan license and lawlessness.

In his stern denunciation of both classes Paul ventures to contrast his own experience and example. In doing so he sets forth the blessedness and inspiration which he has found in fellowship with Christ. In the first chapter of the epistle he has said, "To me to live is Christ," and here he expresses the same thought. In the second chapter he has given Christ as the supreme example of lowly service. Here he pens a passage of incomparable importance concerning his personal relation to his Lord. That paragraph in the second chapter which describes the humiliation and exaltation of Christ and this description of Paul's passion to attain to the likeness of Christ and a full experimental knowledge of him are among the most profound and precious paragraphs which his writings contain.

1. THE TRUE ISRAELITES   Ch. 3:1-3

1 Finally, my brethren, rejoice in the Lord. To write the same things to you, to me indeed is not irksome, but for you it is safe. 2 Beware of the dogs, beware of the evil workers, beware of the concision: 3 for we are the circumcision, who worship by the Spirit of God, and glory in Christ Jesus, and have no confidence in the flesh.

"Finally, my brethren, rejoice in the Lord," writes the apostle. The word "finally" is not to be pressed too far. It may indicate that Paul intended to end his letter just here, but it is not necessary so to suppose. The word may mean "henceforth," or "for the rest," or merely "further." It is quite possible that this familiar formula is used only to introduce what follows. Paul is passing from one topic to another; and in doing so he repeats his familiar exhortation, "Rejoice in the Lord." This already has been found to be the keynote of the epistle. It will be struck repeatedly. Here it introduces a severe rebuke, and when the solemn tones of warning have died away the notes of "joy" and "rejoice" will burst forth again in gladness.

The warning is introduced with the admission that it has been given many times before. Paul declares that he does not hesitate thus to repeat himself because he knows that the matter concerns the safety of his dear friends. "To write the same things to you, to me indeed is not irksome, but for you it is safe." He may refer to other letters written to the Philippians which have been lost, or to similar warnings given when on his visits to Philippi. Paul evidently has cautioned them repeatedly against false teachers who might lead them away from the true gospel of Christ. Thus there is a certain tone of apology as he introduces his subject. However, admonitions are never old until the necessity for them has ceased. Public teachers must often repeat their instructions, even to the point of weariness to themselves and to their hearers; it is wise and necessary for them so to do until their precepts are obeyed, or until the perils pointed out have disappeared.

"Beware of the dogs, beware of the evil workers, beware of the concision." To whom can the apostle be referring in terms so severe?

Some suppose that he had in mind unconverted Jews. Surely he had suffered sufficiently from this source to justify his use of such terms. However, this would be in contradiction to Paul's usual custom. He loved his fellow countrymen. He spoke of them in terms of the utmost affection. He longed for their highest welfare. He was willing to die in their service. There were Jews, however, who professed to believe in Christ but depended for their salvation upon keeping the rites of Judaism. These Judaizers were selfish and bitter and cruel and proud. They went everywhere, stirring up trouble among Christian converts and insisting that unless men kept the law of Moses they could not be saved. Paul regarded their teachings as dangerous, as indeed subversive of the gospel of Christ. For them no words of condemnation could be too severe. In his epistle to the Galatians, and in the closing chapters of his second epistle to the Corinthians, the apostle deals at great length and in terms of unmeasured condemnation with these enemies of Christ.

These seem to be the persons against whom this warning is directed. Here he designates them as "dogs," thus adopting a familiar term of reproach commonly used by Jews to describe Gentiles, and probably used by the Judaizers to express their contempt for Christians who neglected the rites of Judaism. Paul insists that these false teachers are the real "dogs." They have followed Paul, growling, barking, snapping at his heels. However, the title is used by the apostle in the more general sense of their being profane and unclean. As such they have merited the bitter retort hurled back at them by Paul. He further designates them as "evil workers." They are mischief-makers. Not only are they immoral in character, but they are injurious in their influence. They are active, but their activity and zeal make for faction and disorder and unbelief. The term indicates that these persons were in the professing church, and were endangering its very life.

They are called further the "concision." Paul thus parodies the word "circumcision." The false teachers pride themselves upon ceremonies of which this initial rite was the type and chief example. Paul insists that this rite when substituted for faith in Christ, and not accompanied by obedience and love, loses all its meaning. It becomes a mere mutilation.

The same is true of all religious ceremonies. When they cease to express true emotion and belief they become empty forms. One must be careful not to despise rituals and liturgies. They may be of the greatest service, and may stimulate belief and aid devotion. However, when they are divorced from faith and love, and regarded as grounds of salvation, they become an injury and a delusion. This is true, also, of creeds. Christians who accept no prescribed ritual may still be formalists. When the profession of certain doctrines or dogmas is regarded as the essence of religion, when persons expect to be saved by their orthodoxy, when strict adherence to a formula of faith is accompanied by no kindliness of spirit or depth of love, then formalism is seen in its most dangerous and familiar aspect. Externalism in religion was not confined to the first century. Formalism belongs to no one church.

In contrast with the false teachers, who made outward forms essential to salvation and boasted of their loyalty to the law of Moses, Paul declares that those who trust to Christ alone for salvation form the true Israel of God. "We are the circumcision," is the claim. Not an external rite but a cleansing of the heart is the real sign of a right relation to God.

Three proofs are given to support this claim. They form an admirable description of the elements of a normal Christian experience. True Israelites "worship by the Spirit of God." The word for "worship" is one applied to the ritual "service" rendered by the Jews to God as his chosen people. It was expressed in the elaborate ceremonial of the Tabernacle and the Temple, which was but a symbol of all the priestly service the nation was supposed to render to the peoples of the world.

Such a service, not in shadow but in reality, is being rendered by the Christian church, for its service is "by the Spirit of God." It is inspired and guided and supported by his Spirit. No matter how simple or how elaborate the ritual, no matter whether the place be a vast cathedral or a humble home, no matter whether the leader be a cultured ecclesiastic or a crude peasant, the worship is acceptable to God when it is controlled by his Spirit. So it is with the whole liturgy of life. All who are filled with the Holy Spirit are true priests of God, and their simplest tasks may be part of the sacred service they are rendering to a needy world.

They "glory in Christ Jesus." This is in contrast to those who glory in legal observances, or in external ceremonies, as grounds of acceptance with God or as the source of true righteousness. This was the temptation of the Jew; it was the most serious fault of the false teachers who attempted to bind upon the consciences of Christians the ceremonial law of Moses. True believers "glory in Christ Jesus." On the one hand they place no trust in outward rites to secure their salvation; on the other their attitude in reference to Christ is one of exultant confidence. They have a triumphant assurance of his presence, his power, his unfailing grace.

They "have no confidence in the flesh." The term "flesh" denotes all that man is and achieves aside from the Spirit of God. It is defined by all the list of things which follow, and in which Paul once trusted—his legal observance, Jewish descent, social standing, moral attainments. In none of these does a Christian put confidence as he stands before God. He realizes his helplessness, his utter unworthiness, his sin; and he believes that nothing in his character or conduct has attained to the divine standard of righteousness. Then he sees the cross, and then the risen Christ, and he rejoices in all that the Savior has done for him and in all that he is doing still, and he glories in Christ Jesus. This leads him to praise God, and to pray for others, and to render the priestly service of spiritual worship and unselfish living. Thus in experience the order of the three clauses may be reversed. However, they all characterize the life of true believers, who "worship by the Spirit of God, and glory in Christ Jesus, and have no confidence in the flesh."

2. PAUL'S JEWISH PRIVILEGES   Ch. 3:4-7

4 though I myself might have confidence even in the flesh: if any other man thinketh to have confidence in the flesh, I yet more: 5 circumcised the eighth day, of the stock of Israel, of the tribe of Benjamin, a Hebrew of He-

brews; as touching the law, a Pharisee; 6 as touching zeal,
persecuting the church; as touching the righteousness which
is in the law, found blameless. 7 Howbeit what things
were gain to me, these have I counted loss for Christ.

The conversion of Saul of Tarsus and his sudden transformation into a Christian apostle is one of the most surprising miracles in history. It forms, indeed, one of the
strongest arguments in support of belief in the supreme
miracle, namely, the resurrection of Jesus Christ. Unless
on the way to Damascus, Saul met this living Lord, it is
impossible to give a rational explanation of so sudden a
change in all his views of life and its values. He experienced a mental and spiritual revolution. He regarded as
worthless all that before had seemed most precious, and he
became willing to sacrifice his life in a cause which he had
regarded as deserving only of detestation and hate. The
explanation is summed up by the apostle in the single word
"Christ," or, as he affirms, "What things were gain to me,
these have I counted loss for Christ."

This personal experience is cited by Paul to enforce his
warning against the false teachers who have troubled all
the churches he has founded, and now are endangering the
peace of the Christians at Philippi. These Judaizers, while
professing faith in Christ, insist on compelling all Christians to observe the rites of Judaism. Paul has been insisting that true believers place no confidence in these
ceremonies as grounds of salvation. He now gives himself
as an example. In accepting Christ as a personal Savior
he had given up all dependence upon Jewish privileges and
prerogatives as securing for him acceptance with God.
There was a reality in these privileges. There had been an
advantage in being a Jew. Yet such privileges should have
made the Jews messengers of God to the other nations and
should have prepared them to receive Christ, instead of
fostering in them selfishness and bigotry and pride and
spiritual blindness.

Paul fully realizes the value of all that he enjoyed as a

Jew, and he possessed these privileges in a marked degree. So, if anyone should be justified in depending upon such Jewish prerogatives, he is the man. "Though I myself might have confidence even in the flesh:" he writes, referring to all he had received by inheritance and to all that he had attained by personal effort; "if any other man thinketh to have confidence in the flesh, I yet more." He has in mind the false teachers, with their proud claims based on adherence to Jewish rites. If there be any saving value in inherited privileges and in outward ceremonies, Paul is saying, he, and not the Judaizers, is in a position to lay first claim to the boasted advantage.

1. He had been "circumcised the eighth day." He was thus a genuine Jew, and at his birth had been sealed as such by the initial rite, which was administered in infancy and only to such as were of pure blood. He was no proselyte to the faith, but a Jew by birth.

2. He was "of the stock of Israel," that is, a direct descendant of the patriarch Jacob, whose sacred name "Israel," bestowed upon him by God himself, gave to the Jews their cherished name of "Israelites," and designated them as the covenant people of God. They traced their ancestry not only to Abraham, as did also the Ishmaelites, and to Isaac, as did also the Edomites, but to Jacob, who had become "Israel," who had "prevailed" with God, and to whom the chosen people alone owed their origin.

3. "Of the tribe of Benjamin" was a proud claim. Benjamin was a son of Jacob's loved wife, Rachel, and the only one of the sons of Jacob who was born in the Promised Land. From the tribe of Benjamin had come Israel's first king, Saul, whose name had been given to Paul at his birth. The tribe of Benjamin alone remained loyal to Judah when the kingdom was divided, and after the exile, formed with Judah the nucleus of the new nation.

4. Paul further claimed to be "a Hebrew of Hebrews," which means that he was of pure and unmixed Hebrew stock. The term "Hebrew" designated the Jew in contrast

with foreigners; and "a Hebrew of Hebrews" denoted that
both his father and mother belonged to that race. He was
thus a Hebrew son of Hebrew parents.

To all these inherited advantages, Paul now adds those
of personal character and attainment. "As touching the
law, a Pharisee." The reference is to the law of Moses.
Of this law the Pharisees were the most ardent expositors
and defenders. The term here has no tinge of reproach
but of just pride. Pharisees were not all and always hypocrites. Their devotion to an external law tempted them
to become formalists. The enemies of Jesus included
many Pharisees, and they received his just rebuke and condemnation; but as a party they represented the most loyal
and patriotic and conservative of Jews.

Paul was brought up at the feet of a Pharisee, from
whom he received his instruction in the law. He lived in
strict accordance with the tenets of that sect. What he
here justly claims is his unquestioned doctrinal and religious orthodoxy.

"As touching zeal, persecuting the church." In his
eager defense of the national faith Paul had done all in his
power to exterminate Christians. He had breathed
"threatening and slaughter" against them. He had shown
the same cruel and malignant spirit now being manifested
by the false teachers, and toward the same innocent followers of Christ. He had done so "ignorantly in unbelief."
However, his loyalty and devotion to Judaism were unquestioned and were everywhere known.

Lastly, Paul claims that he was, "as touching the righteousness which is in the law, found blameless." This was
not merely a ceremonial righteousness; it included the
moral requirements of the law. Yet it did not correspond
to a divine standard. No one could claim such righteousness. Nor yet was it an inner righteousness, as Paul after-
ward understood and confessed. However, as judged by
men, and in accordance with an external rule, Paul once
regarded himself as "blameless."

All that Paul had inherited and attained, however, seemed to him worthless as a ground of acceptance with God when he found Christ, and in him pardon and peace and new spiritual power. "Howbeit," he writes, "what things were gain to me, these have I counted loss for Christ." The word "gain" is plural. It includes all those separate items he has enumerated of inherited privilege, legal righteousness, and religious zeal. These were good in themselves, but insofar as they led him to build on a false foundation, inasmuch as they kept him from true faith and righteousness, they were counted as "loss."

This change of values was due to his new knowledge of Christ. All that he once regarded as ground of boasting now seems worthless. Christ is now his ground of confidence, his glory, and his joy.

It must not be forgotten that Paul is writing to rebuke the false pride of professed Christians. Their grounds of boasting were not identical with those known in the church today, but they were the same in substance. Race prejudice still exists. One of its strange manifestations has reversed that of the believers who boasted their Jewish descent, and it rejoices in the vaunted superiority of the Gentile to the Jew. There are those, also, who glory in their orthodoxy of belief, no matter how dead that orthodoxy may be. They are proud likewise of their zeal, even though this zeal manifests itself in bitter animosities against fellow members of the church. Others still are staking their hopes of salvation on their self-righteousness, even when, according to any high moral standard, their righteousness is far from faultless.

The one cure for all these false grounds of boasting, the one source of deliverance from all confidence in inherited privilege, in outward ceremonies, and in personal attainment, can be found in Christ. Those who catch a true vision of his divine glory and his saving grace will regard with sympathy all races of men, will manifest love toward their fellow believers, will humbly acknowledge their moral

weakness and imperfection, and will count as loss anything
that keeps them from a fuller knowledge and experience of
Christ.

3. THE KNOWLEDGE OF CHRIST　Ch. 3:8-11

*8 Yea verily, and I count all things to be loss for the ex-
cellency of the knowledge of Christ Jesus my Lord: for
whom I suffered the loss of all things, and do count them
but refuse, that I may gain Christ, 9 and be found in him,
not having a righteousness of mine own, even that which
is of the law, but that which is through faith in Christ, the
righteousness which is from God by faith: 10 that I may
know him, and the power of his resurrection, and the fellowship of his sufferings, becoming conformed unto his
death; 11 if by any means I may attain unto the resurrection from the dead.*

In no other passage of his writings does Paul set forth so
clearly what "the knowledge of Christ" meant to him, as
he does in this impressive paragraph. From some points
of view this may be regarded as the supreme message of
the Epistle to the Philippians. Because of this paragraph,
and related expressions in other parts of the letter, this
has been known as the "Epistle of the Experimental
Knowledge of Christ." For this knowledge of which Paul
writes is a knowledge which is based on experience, a
knowledge which is full and vital and complete. As such
it relates both to the present and to the future. It is both
a present possession and a future hope. It is now experienced in part, and in the life to come it will be made
perfect.

Paul has been warning his readers against certain false
teachers who were disturbing the church by insisting upon
observing Jewish rites as essential to salvation. He has
maintained that he himself possessed in a preeminent degree all the prerogatives and privileges and attainments
of Judaism, but insofar as they kept him from the true

Savior, and offered a false basis for acceptance with God, them he "counted loss for Christ."

"Yea verily," continues the apostle—and these two English words represent a series of Greek particles which indicate the most fervent emotion—"I count all things to be loss for the excellency of the knowledge of Christ Jesus my Lord." He is correcting or expanding his previous statement. Not only his inherited privilege as a Jew and his personal attainments under Jewish law, but "all things," all that he had formerly prized and valued, all that the world had to offer, he counted "to be loss," a real liability, an actual disadvantage, if they stood between himself and Christ, and in comparison with the priceless privilege of knowing Christ as his Savior and Lord.

"For whom I suffered the loss of all things," writes Paul, slightly changing his form of statement. His vision of Christ not only led him to a new estimate of the values of life, but his acceptance of Christ had resulted in the actual loss of everything he formerly had held dear. His becoming a follower of Christ had induced his enemies to strip away from him all that he had prized. He had lost all the world for the sake of Christ. Yet this had not changed his view. Having in mind all that he once loved he writes, "I . . . do count them but refuse, that I may gain Christ."

It is a striking picture. Here is a man seated before a heap of glittering gems. He has admired them and rejoiced in possessing them. Suddenly he sees another prize, and with this in view he looks upon all his previous treasures as "refuse," as worthless rubbish, while he seeks to grasp the new prize and to make it his own.

This grasping of a prize is somewhat the meaning of his words, "That I may gain Christ." What Paul is desiring, what he is increasingly experiencing, is a fuller and fuller apprehension and appreciation of Christ. Already he believes and trusts. However, he has only begun to discover "the unsearchable riches of Christ." There are treasures untold which he is eager to discover and to claim.

Something of what it means to "gain Christ" Paul proceeds to show. He hopes to "be found in him." This does
not mean merely to be so "found" in the Day of Judgment. Paul has in mind a present experience, which is
to continue and is to have its completion at the return of
Christ. However, he desires now to be found "in Christ."
He wishes this vital union now to be actual. He yearns
to discover its reality. In the present as in the future, in
the view of God and of men, and as a definite personal experience, Paul wishes to be "found" in this blessed relation to his living Lord.

One result will be a new and truer righteousness, "not
having a righteousness of mine own, even that which is of
the law, but that which is through faith in Christ, the
righteousness which is from God by faith." Righteousness here includes both a right relation to God and the
right conduct which God requires. Both are provided in
Christ and are received by faith in him. This righteousness Paul mentions in contrast with any real or imaginary
righteousness which he once may have possessed. That
was a righteousness "which is of the law." It came from
law observance. It consisted in obedience to legal rules
and Jewish ceremonials. The righteousness he now prizes
and seeks to possess more fully finds its origin in the grace
of God and is received by faith alone.

There is, however, another aspect of gaining Christ. It
consists in that fuller knowledge of Christ to which he has
already referred. He repeats it with deeper emphasis and
shows the fuller meaning it enfolds: "That I may know
him," he writes with passionate longing. He wishes for a
richer and richer experience in this priceless knowledge.
He wishes to know Christ in a life which is glorious with
all that is good, and free from all that is evil. He wishes
to "live unto righteousness" and to die "unto sins."

Thus he is eager to know more fully "the power of his
resurrection." Paul wants to discover in daily experience
what it is to have a risen Savior, one whose grace is in-

finite. The sense of continual acceptance with God, peace
and purity, new desires for holiness, willingness to serve
others, continual development into the likeness of his Lord,
all this and infinitely more Paul longs to realize in present
personal experience.

Further, Paul wishes to know "the fellowship of his sufferings, becoming conformed unto his death." As he elsewhere expresses it, he wishes to know in personal experience what it is to be "crucified with Christ," or, to use
the words of the Master, to "take up his cross daily" and
follow him. Such fellowship in the sufferings of Christ includes a turning from sin, and the death of self. It may
involve much of hardship for the sake of Christ. For
Paul it finally meant martyrdom.

This absolute submission to the will of Christ cannot be
instantly attained. However complete the surrender, it
must be repeated again and again. It must be, as Paul
and his Master indicated, a continuous process, a deepening experience. Its beginning may be more difficult, more
impressive, more memorable. However, the increasing
knowledge of Christ always means an unceasing fellowship in his sufferings, an increasing conformity to his death.

The result is resurrection, a knowledge of "the power
of his resurrection," a personal and experimental knowledge of that power. "Resurrection" is mentioned by Paul
first, and then "suffering" and "death." This is the true
order. Faith in a risen Christ results in the power to die
to sin and to self. Those who know "the power of his
resurrection" are the ones who are increasingly able to
enter into "the fellowship of his sufferings" and to become
"conformed unto his death."

This knowledge for which Paul yearns is some day to
be complete. His fellowship with Christ and his likeness
to Christ are sometime to be perfect. This will be, as Paul
has before indicated, in the day of Christ's appearing, or,
as represented here, in the day of "resurrection." As to
his attaining that ultimate and final blessedness, Paul

speaks with modesty, not with doubt, as he says with earnest longing, "If by any means I may attain unto the resurrection from the dead." Any implied uncertainty points to Paul's proper lack of confidence in himself, not to any want of trust in the unfailing grace of God. It does indicate, however, no rash confidence. It prepares us for that statement of strenuous endeavor which Paul will proceed to make.

In this present expression he looks forward with glad anticipation to the time when his knowledge of Christ is to be perfect. It will be when Paul has a part in "the resurrection from the dead." This expression is not the same as "the resurrection of the dead." The latter refers to the future resurrection in general. The phrase Paul here uses denotes the resurrection of believers, "the first resurrection," "the resurrection of life," as contrasted with "the resurrection of condemnation." All the blessedness of that day Paul humbly hopes to attain, and the blessedness will consist, in its essence, in an experience already begun, namely, in the complete personal knowledge of Jesus Christ his Lord.

4. Pressing Toward the Goal   Ch. 3:12-16

12 Not that I have already obtained, or am already made perfect: but I press on, if so be that I may lay hold on that for which also I was laid hold on by Christ Jesus. 13 Brethren, I count not myself yet to have laid hold: but one thing I do, forgetting the things which are behind, and stretching forward to the things which are before, 14 I press on toward the goal unto the prize of the high calling of God in Christ Jesus. 15 Let us therefore, as many as are perfect, be thus minded: and if in anything ye are otherwise minded, this also shall God reveal unto you: 16 only, whereunto we have attained, by that same rule *let us walk.*

The formalist is commonly self-satisfied and complacent. His religion consists in performing certain external rites

or else in subscribing to some written creed. Either of
these he can do quite easily and then be content that by
him the demands of his conscience have been fully met.
To Paul the Christian life was something quite different.
It consisted in a personal knowledge of Christ, submission
to his will, trust in him, and in a continuous effort to attain
to his moral perfection.

In describing his experience he uses the familiar figure
of a runner in a race. Paul compares himself with an athlete who was stripped for the contest and straining every
nerve to win the prize. He entered the contest when, near
the city of Damascus, he caught a vision of the risen Lord.
Then he began to run. He has made some progress. He
has not reached the goal. Dismissing from his mind the
stages of the course already run, and bending forward in
an agony of effort, he is endeavoring to grasp that prize
of perfect fellowship with Christ and complete likeness to
him, which he would attain at the resurrection of the just.

"Not that I have already obtained," he writes, referring
to all those high hopes he has previously described, all the
high possibilities in Christian experience, all the moral excellence which would result from a complete knowledge of
Christ. More definitely still he adds, "Or am already
made perfect." Thus explicitly does he disclaim moral and
spiritual perfection. Such high attainment is far beyond
him. Still he is striving for it. "But I press on," he writes,
expressing his eager pursuit of that which is still ahead, "if
so be that I may lay hold on that for which also I was laid
hold on by Christ Jesus." When Christ met Paul on the
Damascus road, when he subsequently transformed him
from a persecutor into an apostle, he had a definite purpose
in view, namely, that Paul might attain perfection. This,
and nothing less than this, was the ideal which Christ had
in mind for Paul; and it is this which Paul is eagerly striving to secure. He is seeking to grasp that for which he
was grasped by Christ. The purpose of his Lord was for
Paul both an encouragement and a stimulus to strenuous

endeavor; yet the more clearly he saw his divine Master, the more conscious he became that he had not attained to his likeness, nor realized in personal experience the fullness of his transforming power. "Brethren," he repeats, "I count not myself yet to have laid hold." He has already disclaimed this attainment. However, here there is a new emphasis—he is contrasting himself with others. Whatever others may claim, whatever experiences theirs may be, for himself he declares that he has not "laid hold" on the prize; he has not attained the perfection which is purposed for him and promised to him by Christ. Just whom Paul had in mind, and with whom he was contrasting himself, may not be certain—probably those false teachers who regarded with such self-complacency their Jewish privileges and personal attainments. In all ages of church history men can be found willing to claim for themselves not only ceremonial righteousness but even moral and spiritual perfection. Their fault is usually due to their failure to know their own hearts or to see the flawless glory of the Lord. Whatever may have been claimed for themselves by others, Paul saw the divine ideal far before him; yet to attain this ideal he was making unceasing endeavor.

To illustrate this effort he employs a figure drawn from the athletic games. It is a familiar figure in the writings of the apostle. As applied by Paul it indicates something of the dignity of the Christian life. It implies not only the manliness and earnestness of such a life but also its glory, for to become a contestant in such games as the Olympic was an honor; to be a victor was to attain deathless fame.

In the use of this figure usually there are at least three points of comparison in the mind of the apostle. The first is singleness of purpose; the second is freedom from encumbering weights; the third is ceaseless exertion. The first is expressed by the phrase, "But one thing I do." This was undoubtedly true of Paul. No other life has been lived with such definiteness of aim; no other career has been run with such unity of purpose. Nothing could distract the apostle. Nothing could divert him from his course. He had set his eye upon the goal placed before him by Christ. To attain it was his single purpose. Upon that goal he concentrated all his thought and his desire.

There is a second requisite for a successful runner. He must strip for the race. He can carry with him no entangling garments. In other references to the race, Christians are urged to "lay aside every weight," and every besetting sin, and to divest themselves of everything which might impede their progress. Here the figure is somewhat altered. Paul declares that he is "forgetting the things which are behind." There are some persons who allow their moral and spiritual progress to be hindered by the burdens of memory. They fix their minds so definitely upon past experiences that they have no strength and no courage for present effort. Here, however, Paul has in mind the fixed purpose of the athlete who keeps his eye intent upon the goal and refuses to look backward. Nothing is more dangerous for a runner than to look behind. He is certain to trip or to lose his stride, to lose speed, possibly to lose courage. Paul dismisses from his mind "the things which are behind." By these he means the stages of the course which he has already run. He entered the race when Christ "laid hold" on him, in the hour of his conversion. He then began to run. Part of the course has been covered. Much lies ahead. He refuses to look at his past attainments. They are probably far greater than those of other Christians, but he dismisses them from his mind. He will not turn his glance backward. His gaze is fixed intently on the part of the course yet to be run. He sees how much remains for him to attain in spiritual life and perfection.

Therefore, he is "stretching forward to the things which are before." He is not relaxing his effort as though, in this present life, he has reached the goal. Rather, like an athlete who is leaning forward in an agony of effort, he is "stretching forward." It is the graphic phrase of the foot race. It indicates the expenditure of every ounce of energy. It pictures the runner in a final agony of effort to win the race.

Again, in a single clause, Paul gathers up the whole meaning of the metaphor: "I press on toward the goal unto the prize of the high calling of God in Christ Jesus." It is needless to distinguish between what is symbolized by the "goal" and the "prize." Both refer to that exalted destiny to which God has summoned the apostle. Possibly, however, the "goal" fixes the thought upon the end of the course, and the "prize" upon the reward which follows. Paul has not yet ceased from effort. He will not until the race is won.

Thus the "prize" for which Paul is striving is no fading garland of leaves; it is the immortal crown of perfect righteousness which will be his when he has attained unto "the resurrection from the dead" at the coming of Christ. It is included in the "high," or "upward" or "heavenly," "calling" which God has given him. This "calling" means the offer of salvation, "the decisive appeal of God to the soul which is made in Christ Jesus."

To this call Paul has responded; and he is running with patience the race that is set before him. Conscious that he is still far from the goal, he is agonizing in an effort for daily progress, believing that some day he will receive the prize, for his trust is in Christ Jesus, through whom his "high calling" has come and by whose grace its glorious possibilities will be attained.

Paul regards this consciousness of moral and spiritual imperfection, and this determination to make continual moral and spiritual progress, as the very mark and proof of Christian maturity.

"Let us therefore," he concludes, "as many as are perfect, be thus minded." Paul uses the word "perfect" in a different sense from that of the earlier phrase (v. 12). It here denotes those who are "mature." He wishes to describe those who, as Christians, are "fullgrown" men, as contrasted with "babes in Christ." It indicates a relative "perfection," as that of an adult compared with that of an infant. Paul means that all persons who know the real nature and demands of the Christian life should share his attitude of mind and should imitate his effort. One evidence of spiritual immaturity is the claim of spiritual perfection. Those who know Christ best are most conscious of the many stages yet to be run before they attain the goal. Those who understand most fully the high demands of the Christian ideal are making the most earnest effort toward spiritual progress.

There were evidently some in Philippi who needed this caution. There are some in the church today. Spiritual pride is subtle and probably much more common than is supposed. It is the essential fault of the formalist and the Pharisee. However, there are many Christians so immature as to thank God that they are not as other men, and so spiritually childish as to suppose that they need not forget their past attainments, and need not daily "press . . . toward the goal."

Of such persons Paul speaks with much gentleness and forbearance. One always should. Not all formalists are hypocrites. Many are self-deceived. Many are real "babes in Christ," who only need further spiritual development and enlightenment. "If in anything ye are otherwise minded," writes Paul, "this also shall God reveal unto you." There are probably those in Philippi who are really sincere but who do not agree with Paul in all that he has said about perfection or in all that he feels about the need of continual spiritual progress. Paul will be patient with such. Further enlightenment will come to them. God will "reveal," will "unveil" the truth. He will correct their fault. He will give them more perfect light. There is, however, one condition which must be fulfilled. We must live up to the light we have. "Only," Paul insists, referring to this condition, "whereunto we have attained, by that same rule let us walk." We must deal kindly with one another. There are probably many different standards of perfection. If we attain our present standard and keep our eyes on Christ, we shall probably find that there remains much to be desired, much to be attained. It is well, therefore, to heed the advice of Paul, which has been rendered, "If we are to make progress, we must live up to our best present knowledge of the ideals and requirement of the Christian life."

B. AGAINST LAWLESSNESS Ch. 3:17-21

17 Brethren, be ye imitators together of me, and mark them that so walk even as ye have us for an ensample. 18 For many walk, of whom I told you often, and now tell you even weeping, that they are the enemies of the cross of Christ: 19 whose end is perdition, whose god is the belly, and whose glory is in their shame, who mind earthly things. 20 For our citizenship is in heaven; whence also we wait for a Saviour, the Lord Jesus Christ: 21 who shall fashion anew the body of our humiliation, that it may be conformed to the body of his glory, according to the working whereby he is able even to subject all things unto himself.

The church of Christ has always been troubled by legalists. These men have made salvation depend upon the observance of rites, upon subscription to a creed, or upon the performance of good deeds. However, the life of the church has likewise been endangered by those who in doctrine or in practice have confused liberty with license. These men have taught that salvation by grace means freedom to live in sin, and deliverance from the law as a ground of acceptance with God means that in daily practice a Christian may live in disregard of the requirements and demands of the law and still escape the just judgment of God.

Against such men Paul solemnly warns his readers. In contrast with these libertines he mentions himself as an example of true Christian living. He is not to be accused of being proud or self-conscious. It must not be forgotten that he has been admitting his own lack of perfection. He confesses that he is far from the goal. Yet he is striving to attain the true ideal which Christ has placed before him. It is not self-conceit, but rather conscious sincerity which enables him to say, "Brethren, be ye imitators together of me." From all that he has said, he evidently does not regard himself as faultless. He wishes his readers to follow him only insofar as he is following Christ. Yet in his earnest effort to become like his Lord, and in his long life of ceaseless activity, it is true that he has been so consistent that he can fearlessly ask others to imitate him. Nor does he claim to be alone worthy of imitation. There are those at Philippi who are following Christ even as Paul is. "Mark them that so walk," he writes, "even as ye have us for an ensample." In the first clause he says, "Be ye imitators together of me." Here he says, "Even as ye have us for an ensample." He changes from "me" to "us," with evident intent. With himself he unites Timothy and Epaphroditus, who have been mentioned as men whose lives are marked not by self-gratification but by self-sacrifice. Thus, upon Paul and his companions and upon the many in Philippi who are living similar lives, the readers are urged earnestly to fix their attention as upon men who are safe guides for Christian conduct.

There are men of very different character. Against their influence Paul proceeds to give a most solemn warning. "For many walk, of whom I told you often, and now tell you even weeping." These are evidently members of the church. Paul's tears are a proof of this. It breaks his heart to know of men who profess Christ with their lips and deny him with their lives. He declares that there are many such, and that he frequently has been compelled to warn the Philippians against their influence. This warning he now repeats, with deep emotion.

"They are the enemies of the cross of Christ," he writes.

Their enmity is not that of false doctrine. This would have been true of the "formalists," the Judaizers, whom Paul has rebuked in the paragraphs which precede, who make the cross of no effect by their teaching. These men, however, are enemies of the central principle of the Christian life. The cross is the very symbol of death to self and to sin. "If any man would come after me, let him deny himself, and take up his cross, and follow me," were the significant words of the Master. By their sensual self-indulgence these men are bringing into disrepute the cross and all the sacred realities the cross is known to represent.

"Whose end is perdition," Paul declares. He means that the issue of their conduct will be complete moral ruin. In Paul's language "perdition" is the exact opposite of "salvation." It does not mean annihilation, but the loss of all that makes for true life, both now and in the world to come. These men are "doomed to destruction." Their "god is the belly"; that is, in their grossness the real objects of their worship are the lower appetites of the body. They are devotees of the sensual nature. Their "glory is in their shame," since they pride themselves upon those indulgences which are really their disgrace. Their boasted liberty is bondage to lust.

"Who mind earthly things" is a phrase which not only gives another ground of condemnation but points to the very source of their depravity. Their thoughts, their feelings, their interests are fixed solely upon the things of this present life. Their horizon is limited to the things of time and of sense. Their efforts are confined to the dust and dross of earth.

In striking contrast with these false followers of Christ, whose lives and aims indicate that they belong wholly to the world of sense and time, Paul describes true Christians as being citizens of a heavenly commonwealth: "For our citizenship is in heaven." This metaphor the Philippians would fully appreciate. As inhabitants of a Roman colony they enjoyed Roman citizenship. They might never have

seen the Imperial City, but they were under its protection
and lived according to its laws and enjoyed the privileges
of its residents. So Christians form "a colony of heaven."
They are under its care. To it they owe their allegiance.
In its register their names are enrolled. Their conduct is
regulated by its laws. Their hopes are centered on its
glories.

"Whence also we wait for a Saviour," writes the apostle.
Of that heavenly commonwealth Christ is the King. Some
day he is to appear. "We wait" for him. The word implies eager longing, earnest expectation, fervent desire.
That he will come in his own lifetime Paul is not certain.
He rather thinks that he will die before his Lord's return.
He hopes, however, that he may live until Christ shall appear and thus never experience death. His attitude should
be that of all believers. The coming of Christ may be in
the lifetime of any generation; no one can affirm that it
will or that it will not. His return is the blessed hope of
the church. Sometimes that hope grows dim. Then
worldliness increases, and Christians "mind earthly things."
Citizens of the heavenly commonwealth should eagerly
look for "a Saviour," even "the Lord Jesus Christ."

Something of his saving power they have already realized. When he appears their salvation will be complete.
It will include the transformation of the body. He "shall
fashion anew the body of our humiliation." The false believers whom Paul has been describing make the gratification of bodily appetites the very end and aim of life. True
believers, on the other hand, are not to despise the body.
It is worthy of all honor and care as the instrument of the
soul, and as the temple of the Holy Spirit. At present
the body is exposed to passion, suffering, and pain. It is
subject to sickness, weakness, and death. However, there
awaits it a glorious destiny. When Christ comes he will
"fashion anew the body of our humiliation, that it may be
conformed to the body of his glory."

Just what the nature of this glorified body is to be no

one can conjecture. It is to be immortal and the fit instrument of the perfected spirit. In some inscrutable way it is to retain its identity with "the body of our humiliation." Yet it is not to be the same in substance. "Flesh and blood cannot inherit the kingdom of God." Its type and pattern is the glorified body of the Savior himself. When Christ appears, the bodies of the dead are not merely to be resuscitated, nor are the bodies of the living to be destroyed. To both can be applied these words of the apostle, that Christ "shall fashion [them] anew," that they "may be conformed to the body of his glory." These words are not enough to satisfy our curiosity, but they may suffice to inspire comfort and to stimulate hope.

As the image of the transformed body is that of the ascended Christ, so the power of the transformation is "the working whereby he is able even to subject all things unto himself." The fashioning anew of the body of believers is thus only a part of the gracious redeeming purpose of Christ. "All things" are to be made subject to his sovereign will, all things to share in the glory of his resurrection victory. Such glorious promises should make us less intent upon "earthly things," more eager to set our affections on things above, more mindful of our citizenship in heaven, "whence also we wait for a Saviour, the Lord Jesus Christ."

VI
PAUL'S FRIENDS IN PHILIPPI
Ch. 4:1-3

1 Wherefore, my brethren beloved and longed for, my joy and crown, so stand fast in the Lord, my beloved.

2 I exhort Euodia, and I exhort Syntyche, to be of the same mind in the Lord. 3 Yea, I beseech thee also, true yokefellow, help these women, for they labored with me in the gospel, with Clement also, and the rest of my fellow-workers, whose names are in the book of life.

A certain general order of thought is being followed even in this informal, friendly epistle. Paul first writes of his personal experiences in Rome, and then adds certain pertinent exhortations to his readers. He next mentions the plans of Timothy and Epaphroditus, who are sharing his imprisonment, and then warns the Philippians against the evil influence of certain men of a very different character, who may mislead them by their erroneous teaching or by their immoral conduct. He now turns to mention the names of certain individuals in the Philippian church, and to urge them to live in Christian harmony. This personal appeal is directly connected with the great truths set forth in the previous paragraph. At least it is introduced by a touching exhortation based upon those truths. "Wherefore, my brethren," writes Paul, "so stand fast in the Lord." He is saying in effect that, in view of his own example, and further in view of their heavenly citizenship and their glorious hopes, they must be loyal and steadfast; they must be true to their Christian ideals and profession.

The appeal is most affectionate. He addresses his readers as "brethren," and twice he repeats the word "beloved." He declares that these "brethren beloved" are "longed for"; they are in his heart and mind, and his separation from them causes him pain and distress; he yearns to see them. He calls them his "joy and crown." They are such now. In fullest measure they will be such at the return of Christ. Even in the present time they are a source of true gladness, and they are the badge and proof of his devoted service. However, at the appearing of Christ, these faithful converts will be the occasion of deepest satisfaction. They will be the witnesses to his triumphant career. The "crown" refers to the wreath of laurel, bay, or pine, which was placed upon the brow of a victor in the games; so, in the day of final rewards, these steadfast Christians will attest the fact that Paul "did not run in vain neither labor in vain." The same truth is expressed more fully in an earlier letter written to a church in the neighboring city of Thessalonica: "What is our hope, or joy, or crown of glorying? Are not even ye, before our Lord Jesus at his coming? For ye are our glory and our joy."

This tender and loving appeal must have inspired the readers to higher and more steadfast devotion; but it also serves to introduce the delicate matter to which Paul now turns. He has learned that a disagreement has arisen between two members of the church at Philippi, and in writing this letter he takes occasion to urge them to resolve their differences in a manner becoming to true Christians; and he further urges one of his own trusted companions to assist in effecting the reconciliation. The two members at variance were women. Their beautiful Greek names might have forecast a more fragrant memory in the history of the early church. One was Euodia, "Prosperous Journey," or according to some texts, "Sweet Savor," or "Fragrance." The other was Syntyche, "Good Fortune," "Fortunate," or "Affable." Both were evidently women of high standing who had been of great service in furthering the establishment of the church in Philippi.

The cause of their dissension is unknown. Nor is it a

matter of importance.   Some think that it was a difference
as to doctrine, especially the doctrine of Christian perfection which Paul has just discussed.   It is true that this particular doctrine has been a ground of disagreement among
believers even in recent years.   It is also true that certain
admirable Christians who have claimed something like sin-
lessness have shown a spirit which to others has seemed to
fall short of perfection.

More probably the very energy and activity of these two
devoted women may have occasioned some accidental fric-
tion, and they had not managed the difficulty wisely.   They
had allowed the discord to deepen into dislike and distrust
and the estrangement had become fixed and permanent.

However, the situation was not so deplorable as some
have supposed.   There are interpreters who hold Euodia
and Syntyche responsible for every imperfection which
existed in the Philippian church.   It is, however, very
improbable that these worthy women should be asked to
bear so heavy a burden of blame.   Paul does urge his
readers, in other parts of this letter, to cultivate a spirit of
harmony.   He even gives a passionate plea for unity.
However, the most that should be said is that the dissension between these two workers was the most marked disagreement which had arisen among the body of believers
in Philippi.

In any case the matter was serious enough to require
special mention and even this rather public admonition by
Paul.   The matter is handled by the apostle with marked
courtesy and wisdom.   "I exhort Euodia, and I exhort
Syntyche," he writes, using the same word in each case
and mentioning the names in alphabetical order, thus
showing absolute impartiality.   The exhortation, "To be
of the same mind in the Lord," indicates that the desired
agreement should be sought on the highest ground and
from the loftiest motives.   They should remember their
common relation to Christ and to his church.   As Christian
sisters they should put aside all jealousy and ill will, and,

in a spirit of humility and charity, should resolve to understand each other and to seek for mutual amity and peace.

Paul further proposes that a trusted friend may act as
an arbiter and peacemaker: "Yea, I beseech thee also,
true yokefellow, help these women," that is to say, help
them to compose their differences. Whom Paul designates
as his "yokefellow," no one knows. The Greek word is
σύνζυγε. Many believe it is to be regarded as a proper
name and suppose that Paul is saying to his friend, "Act
according to your name; show yourself to be a true yokefellow, one who will unite those who are separated." It is
more probable, however, that "yokefellow" is a common
noun, referring to some member of the Philippian church,
or even to some companion of Paul. Much could be said
in favor of the conjecture that the one designated was
"Luke, the beloved physician," whose home is supposed
to have been in Philippi.

Evidently the person in mind was a man of rare discre-
tion. His task was delicate, as can easily be imagined.
However, it was noble and honorable. A sympathetic
friend can do much to reconcile difficulties between Christians. The ministry of reconciliation is much needed and
is an exalted form of service. "Blessed are the peace-
makers."

The reason given to this peacemaker for undertaking his
important task is the high merit and honorable service of
the two women who have become estranged. "For they
labored with me in the gospel," Paul states, reminding his
trusted representative of the devoted help which these
women gave, probably in those early days of the founding
of the Philippian church.

The very thought of these women, and of that time of
earnest, successful Christian effort, brings to Paul's mind
other persons worthy of special mention. One of these
was Clement, of whom nothing further is known. Honor
enough it is for him to be thus named. There were others,
too, whom the apostle does not designate; but with them

Euodia and Syntyche had been associated as helpers of
Paul. He describes them as "the rest of my fellow-
workers, whose names are in the book of life." Paul seems
to say: "Their names need not be included in this letter.
They are written on an imperishable page. They are in
the 'book of life.'" This last phrase is a New Testament
expression which seems to embody the figurative conception of a roll or register of all who share eternal life
through faith in Christ. Their "names are written in
heaven." Possibly, as here used by Paul, the phrase indicates that these beloved "fellow-workers" are no longer
alive. However, living or dead, they form a memorable
company of immortals who have been associated with Paul
in establishing the church of Christ. As Euodia and Syntyche hold an honorable place in that illustrious company,
it is worth the effort of Paul's "true yokefellow" to do anything in his power to bring them into Christian agreement,
and it is only just that they shall be remembered, not simply for their unfortunate dissension, but rather as two
saints of God who have strengthened and supported the
great apostle by their devoted service to the cause of
Christ.

VII
FINAL ADMONITIONS
Ch. 4:4-9

*4 Rejoice in the Lord always: again I will say, Rejoice.
5 Let your forbearance be known unto all men. The Lord
is at hand. 6 In nothing be anxious; but in everything by
prayer and supplication with thanksgiving let your requests
be made known unto God. 7 And the peace of God, which
passeth all understanding, shall guard your hearts and your
thoughts in Christ Jesus.*

*8 Finally, brethren, whatsoever things are true, whatso-
ever things are honorable, whatsoever things are just,
whatsoever things are pure, whatsoever things are lovely,
whatsoever things are of good report; if there be any virtue, and if there be any praise, think on these things. 9
The things which ye both learned and received and heard
and saw in me, these things do: and the God of peace shall
be with you.*

This epistle may be regarded as consisting of three cycles
of personal references, each of which is followed by a
series of practical exhortations. The first of these references is to Paul's own experiences in Rome. The second
is to his companions in imprisonment, Timothy and Epaphroditus. The third is to his friends in Philippi. This
last is specifically a plea to two Christian women, urging
them to compose the differences which had divided them.
Paul now adds certain exhortations addressed to the whole
church. The first of these is an exhortation to "rejoice."
It may possibly be related in thought to the dissension between Euodia and Syntyche, for nothing so surely destroys
gladness of heart as contention and misunderstanding.
However, it is more probable that Paul is now turning, in

this last series of admonitions, to give his readers an informal summary of the whole philosophy and spirit and conduct of Christian life.

These admonitions are presented in two separate paragraphs, one of which makes prominent "the peace of God" (vs. 4-7); the other reaches its climax with the phrase, "the God of peace" (vs. 8-9). These two phrases are quite distinct. The former is shown to be the result of believing prayer. The latter designates the source of spiritual power. The first paragraph is an exhortation to joyfulness and trust. The second is an exhortation to high thinking and noble endeavor.

"Rejoice in the Lord always: again I will say, Rejoice." Thus insistently does Paul sound what his readers now recognize as the keynote of his inspired composition. It expresses the prevailing mood of his own life. It proclaims the ideal for every follower of Christ. Paul insists that joy is not to be an occasional experience, and for exceptional people. All those Philippian Christians are to rejoice, and to rejoice "always." As though realizing that this "always" will include times of darkness as well as of light, times of pain as well as of pleasure, Paul repeats the word with new emphasis, "Again I will say, Rejoice."

It would be a mere mockery to urge any person to rejoice always, or even to exhort some persons to rejoice at any time, were it not for the supreme and essential words, "In the Lord." Abiding joy is possible only in view of all a man has and may have because of his relation to the Lord Jesus Christ. "In the Lord" he has peace with God and victory over temptation and companionship in trial and assured hope for the life to come. If a person is not rejoicing, it is because he is not appropriating to his personal needs all the available riches of grace in Christ Jesus.

One cause of joylessness is the memory of past failures and faults. Added to regret and self-reproach and remorse there is the haunting fear of coming defeat. We are slow

to believe in divine forgiveness, or to expect victory where
once we have been overcome. As Christians the recollection of the past should make us humble in the present and
guard us against self-confidence in the future; but if we believe anything, we surely should believe in the pardoning
love of God and in the power which makes us "more than
conquerors" in Christ.

Another cause of gloom is found in natural temperament
or disposition. Some have a genius for gladness. Others
are continually inclined to take dark views of life; their
humor is seldom cheerful. They are almost proud that
they are pessimists. It is well to remember that dispositions may be controlled and cultivated. Melancholy may
be a fault as well as a misfortune. All should endeavor to
cultivate the fine art of good cheer. Here the help of Christ
is indispensable. "The fruit of the Spirit is . . . joy."
Some people are so constitutionally morose that for them
gladness would be almost a miracle. That miracle they
should expect. They should believe it possible for themselves to "rejoice in the Lord."

Then again, circumstances are sometimes inevitably de-
pressing. Yet it is the very glory of a Christian that he becomes so superior to his surroundings that he is radiantly
cheerful in times of greatest trial and distress. The gladness of his soul is not dependent upon natural conditions.
The man who sounded the stirring challenge, "Rejoice in
the Lord," was a prisoner, bound by a chain to his guard,
poor and lonely and in danger of death, yet triumphant,
exultant, and glad in the fellowship and service of Christ.

Furthermore there is no doubt that sympathy with others
constantly shadows our souls. We feel it selfish to be
happy when so many others are in deep distress. Surely,
no Christian is justified in being indifferent to the suffering
which is about him or in forgetting those less favored than
himself. However, he should remember that gloom and
hopelessness will not prove helpful to those in need. The
greater the darkness, the more will men appreciate cheer

and confidence, Christian faith and Christian hope. A spirit of gladness is the best equipment for a person who would minister to the sorrowing and who seeks to lift burdens from heavy hearts.

To "rejoice in the Lord" does not mean that a man is to be insensible to sorrow and distress, to suffering and to sin, either in his own life or in the lives about him; but it does mean that these dark realities will not be allowed to master him or to blind him to the radiance which streams from the face of his living Lord. Faith in Christ and obedience to him are the sources of abiding joy. Blessed are those who realize that true joy cannot be found aside from him and his holy will. Blessed, too, are those who have discovered "the sacred duty of being happy," and who are seeking with divine aid to "rejoice in the Lord always."

Joy is closely related to gentleness. One whose own heart is ever singing will not usually be harsh and ungracious toward his fellow men. Thus the exhortation to rejoice is followed by the admonition, "Let your forbearance be known unto all men." The word translated "forbearance" has been rendered by various terms, such as "moderation," "gentleness," "consideration for others," and possibly best by the familiar phrase "sweet reasonableness." It describes that courtesy and graciousness which should characterize a Christian gentleman. The term indicates something of "the power of yielding," the ability to give way to the wishes of others, the poise of soul which enables one to sacrifice his own rights, not by necessity but out of generosity and sympathy. It is the opposite of stubbornness and thoughtlessness. It underlies chivalry and true politeness. It was embodied in the man Jesus Christ, whom Paul mentions in another place as the supreme example of "meekness and gentleness." It is described by that "love" which "suffereth long, and is kind," which "envieth not," which "seeketh not its own."

This sweet reasonableness is to be known unto "all

men." This is the difficult part of the exhortation. It would be quite easy to be considerate and kind and gentle toward some persons. There are others, however, toward whom it is difficult to show such a spirit. All persons are not equally amiable. The hard task, the real test, is to show this sweet reasonableness toward the perverse, the thankless, and the unkind. To rejoice "always" is followed by the command to be gentle and forbearing to "all men."

The reason and motive is at once added, "The Lord is at hand." This expression was almost a watchword among the early Christians. Paul uses it also in the Aramaic form, *"Marana tha,"* "O Lord, come!" (I Cor. 16:22). The expectation of the early return of Christ was urged as an incentive to all the Christian virtues. So here, a man could afford to yield his rights to others, for the true Judge was to appear soon. In the glory of his return, human distinctions and differences would seem insignificant and trifling. As those who were to reign with him, Christians could now afford to be gracious and courteous and kind, even toward those who made unfair demands and seemed hardly worthy of respect. This hope of the return of Christ, as an event which might occur in any generation, has been dimmed in the passing centuries. Wherever it is revived and professed one should expect to find a spirit of forbearance and Christian love.

"In nothing be anxious," Paul adds, and his exhortation may be connected with the words which precede. If "the Lord is at hand," why should one worry? His speedy return should not only inspire gentleness but should banish harassing care. More probably the exhortation should be connected with the words which follow. If so, Paul is intimating that the cure for anxiety is to be found in believing prayer. Instead of worrying, which all persons deplore but few escape, Paul urges his readers to find peace of heart by turning to God and seeking fellowship with him. "In everything by prayer and supplication . . . let your

requests be made known unto God." Thus again Paul
employs a universal term. Just as we are to rejoice "always," to be gracious to "all men," so here, "in everything" we are to find relief in prayer. Nothing is too great
for God's power, nothing too small to be beyond his
care. "Prayer" here expresses the general act of devotion; "supplication," the cry of conscious need; "requests,"
the actual favors which are asked of God.

All is to be done in a spirit of gratitude. It is to be
"with thanksgiving." This implies submission, which is
indeed one of the vital elements or conditions of prayer.
Thus, as Paul's words have been rendered, Christians are
to be "anxious in nothing, prayerful in everything, thankful for anything."

A blessed result is sure to follow: "The peace of God,
which passeth all understanding, shall guard your hearts
and your thoughts in Christ Jesus." The word "guard"
indicates that Paul is here employing a military figure,
even to express the power of spiritual peace. There is a
peace which God gives, which he alone can bestow, which
indeed he is ever ready to grant to those who take their
anxieties to him in prayer. This peace "passeth all understanding"; it is far beyond our fondest hopes and brightest
dreams. This peace stands as a sentinel to guard those
who are "in Christ Jesus." For true believers, who are
taking "everything to God in prayer," Christ is the Citadel,
the Fortress of rest. Or, the peace which God gives is
like the garrison of a Greek city, which kept order within
the city and protected the city from hostile foes. So the
"hearts and . . . thoughts" of Christians, all their affections, their desires, their minds, their wills are under the
constant keeping and care of God. His peace guards as a
sentinel, or protects as a garrison, those who are "in Christ
Jesus."

In his philosophy of life, Paul regarded divine and human action as inseparable. He believed in the sovereignty
of God and also in the freedom and responsibility of man.

He could say to the Philippians, "Work out your own salvation . . . for it is God who worketh in you." He did
not attempt to solve the mystery of this relationship. He
always assumed it as an axiom. Thus, in his closing exhortations, when he has insisted that, if his readers have
faith and resort to prayer, the peace which God gives will
guard their hearts and minds, he proceeds at once to insist
that his readers must do their part by controlling their
minds and thoughts. The paragraph which enjoins trust
in God is thus followed by an exhortation to high thinking and noble effort. "Finally, brethren," writes Paul,
probably indicating that he is bringing his epistle to a close,
"whatsoever things are true, whatsoever things are honorable, whatsoever things are just, whatsoever things are
pure, whatsoever things are lovely, whatsoever things are
of good report; if there be any virtue, and if there be any
praise, think on these things."

The opinion has been expressed that Paul speaks here
more like a pagan philosopher than like a Christian apostle. Others go so far as to say that Paul is urging his
readers to consider and appreciate all that is best and
noblest in the pagan life around them. It is true that the
moral ideals here presented include practically all that was
of value in ancient ethics. Yet the Christian character of
the exhortation is evident from the reference to the "peace
of God" which precedes, and to the "God of peace"
which follows, as well as from the higher values which are
given here, as in his other writings, to the very terms which
were familiar to the ancient moralists. Nor are these terms
used by Paul to present an exhaustive list of Christian virtues. He rather is giving certain specific aspects of the
ideal life which Christians should keep in mind and seek
to reproduce.

He would have them consider "whatsoever things are
true." This includes not only veracity and fidelity, but
everything in motive and conduct which corresponds to
the divine ideal revealed in Christ. The moral standards

of Christianity depend upon great realities. They are neither false nor unreliable. They are to be traced back to the very nature of God.

"Whatsoever things are honorable" denotes those things which are morally attractive, which call forth love, which win and charm by their graciousness, which are "amiable" and "winsome" in character.

"Whatsoever things are of good report," or of "good repute," describes such actions and moral qualities as are "fair-sounding" and "high-toned," ringing true to the highest standards of Christian life.

These phrases are followed by two comprehensive clauses which include the whole realm of Christian morality: "If there be any virtue, and if there be any praise"; that is to say, "Whatever moral excellence exists, and whatever praise it deserves." "Praise" does not mean only the commendation of others; nor does it denote merely that which is worthy of praise; rather it describes moral approbation, whether of conscience, or of men, or even of God.

The exhortation is to "think on these things." One must "take account of" them, in estimating the values of life. The mind must be made to dwell upon these high moral ideals, upon things honorable and just and pure and lovely and of good report, upon true virtue and the praise it deserves.

Such high thinking cannot fail to result in nobility of character and in worthy deeds, for "as [a man] . . . thinketh within himself, so is he." Nothing can be of greater vital importance than a proper control of thought. The objects on which a man allows his mind habitually to dwell determine his acts, his career, his destiny.

However, Paul adds an exhortation dealing specifically with Christian conduct and practice: "The things which ye both learned and received and heard and saw in me, these things do." Right thinking is invaluable, but it must also be accompanied by resolution; it must be followed by determined action. All the high ideals that Paul has just reviewed, all the precepts for life and service which he previously has given to his readers, all the things that they have "learned and received," they must do.   Yet Paul has given them not only his inspired instruction but also his inspiring example: they must do the things that they "heard and saw" in him when he was present with them.

This exhortation is accompanied by an encouraging promise, "And the God of peace shall be with you."   The former promise was that "the peace of God" would guard them.   Here the assurance is that "the God of peace" will be with them.   This must mean, not merely that God will be present, but that he will manifest his presence; not only that he will be with them, but that he will be gracious toward them, and that, too, in his specific character as "the God of peace"; that is, he will give them peace and will establish their minds in right thinking and will aid them in every high and noble endeavor.

VIII
PAUL'S EXPRESSION
OF THANKS
Ch. 4:10-20

10 But I rejoice in the Lord greatly, that now at length ye have revived your thought for me; wherein ye did indeed take thought, but ye lacked opportunity. 11 Not that I speak in respect of want: for I have learned, in whatsoever state I am, therein to be content. 12 I know how to be abased, and I know also how to abound: in everything and in all things have I learned the secret both to be filled and to be hungry, both to abound and to be in want. 13 I can do all things in him that strengtheneth me. 14 Howbeit ye did well that ye had fellowship with my affliction. 15 And ye yourselves also know, ye Philippians, that in the beginning of the gospel, when I departed from Macedonia, no church had fellowship with me in the matter of giving and receiving but ye only; 16 for even in Thessalonica ye sent once and again unto my need. 17 Not that I seek for the gift; but I seek for the fruit that increaseth to your account. 18 But I have all things, and abound: I am filled, having received from Epaphroditus the things that came from you, an odor of a sweet smell, a sacrifice acceptable, well-pleasing to God. 19 And my God shall supply every need of yours according to his riches in glory in Christ Jesus. 20 Now unto our God and Father be the glory for ever and ever. Amen.

The first purpose of Paul in writing this epistle is to express his gratitude for the gifts sent to him by his Philippian friends. This subject, however, is the last to be reached. To Paul this matter is not the first in importance. His own physical comfort is of far less concern to him than is the spiritual welfare of his readers. He has referred earlier to their kindness. The whole letter expresses his appreciation of their love. However, the last place in the letter is the place of greatest prominence. All that has preceded has only prepared the minds of his readers for the message which forms the climax of the epistle. This message of thanks is a rare blending of affection, of dignity, of delicacy, with a certain undertone of gentle pleasantry. It is an embodiment of ideal Christian courtesy.

"But I rejoice in the Lord greatly," writes Paul, striking for the last time the keynote of the epistle, with the new emphasis of the word "greatly." However, his joy is, as ever, "in the Lord," for he recognizes that the motive which has prompted the gift is Christian love, and that Christ himself has inspired their sympathy and is the ultimate source of their gift.

His joy is due to the fact "that now at length ye have revived your thought for me." Some time evidently had elapsed since he had received a remembrance from them. Now, however, they have "revived" their thought, or, as otherwise rendered, "You have revived your drooping remembrance of me." Possibly, however, "revived" means more exactly "caused to sprout and bloom" like a tree in springtime. The winter of their long silence has ended. Their message and their gifts are fragrant blossoms, the perfume and the beauty of which gladden his heart.

However, Paul would not even hint that his friends had forgotten him. He hastens to say that what they lacked was not sympathy but the chance of showing it: "Wherein ye did indeed take thought, but ye lacked opportunity." They may have been ignorant, for some time, as to Paul's imprisonment. They may have found it difficult to send a messenger. He assures them that he has no doubt of their continual concern for him and of their constant desire to grant him any possible relief.

Nor does he wish to complain of his need. Their gift was timely. He had been in distress; but he did not intend

to allude to this. He would not have his expression of
gratitude so understood: "Not that I speak in respect of
want." Under no circumstances would he express discontent; nor would he so express his thanks as to seem to
be requesting another gift. "For I have learned," he explains, "in whatsoever state I am, therein to be content."
There is no more difficult lesson to be learned. For Paul
it has been a matter of long tuition. The school of discipline has included many difficult courses. Some of these
Paul now specifies.

"I know how to be abased." He knows it as the result
of actual experience. He has felt the humiliation of abject
poverty. "I know also how to abound." He knows what
it means to have all needs supplied. "In everything and
in all things," that is, in all conditions and under all circumstances, "have I learned the secret both to be filled
and to be hungry, both to abound and to be in want."
Paul is indulging in no mere metaphor when he speaks of
hunger and want. Again and again, in his devoted service,
he has been without food or shelter and has suffered anguish because denied the actual necessities of life. Yet he
has learned the secret of being content under all these
conditions.

The phrase "Learned the secret" originally meant "In-
itiated into the secret." The word was used of initiation
into the Greek Mysteries. Here it has lost much of its
original force. However, it still indicates a process involv-
ing much of hardship and of discipline. Quite truly, however, this ability to rise above all circumstances is the great
secret of Paul's life.

It is to be noted that Paul says nothing foolish about
poverty's being a great blessing. He has learned, however,
that even the poor man does not lack those things which
are essential to the highest life. Nor does he say anything
about riches being a great curse. He does not intimate
that the only thing to do with wealth is to abandon it.
This might be the cowardly evasion of real responsibility.

He does claim, however, to have learned the secret of being cheerful and joyful even in times of penury and privation, of being generous and unselfish and grateful in seasons of prosperity and of abundance.

Nor does Paul mean that he has become an unfeeling fatalist or a stoic. There is such a thing as "divine discontent." Conditions may exist indifference to which would be sinful. To be satisfied with one's own imperfections, to be unconcerned when others are in misery and distress, to be at ease while the great world is ignorant of the gospel of grace—such is not the contentment of Paul. He is ceaselessly struggling for spiritual progress; his tears are flowing in sympathy for human need; he is pouring out his life in service for his Lord. However, he is able to be calm and confident in the midst of the most disturbing circumstances. More particularly, he has refused to allow his peace and joy to be dependent upon material possessions and upon physical comforts. He will not allow his spirit to be chained by the satisfactions of the body. He would not choose or enjoy hunger and want, imprisonment and pain; yet, in the midst of these, he can sing his song of triumph and of praise.

The secret of such contentment is Christ, or Paul's relation to Christ. Paul is abiding in Christ. He regards himself as "in Christ." "I can do all things," he declares, "in him that strengtheneth me." This is possibly the supreme and comprehensive message of this chapter. In the first chapter the message was, "For to me to live is Christ"; in the second it was, "Have this mind in you, which was also in Christ Jesus"; in the third, "I press on toward the goal unto the prize of the high calling of God in Christ Jesus." These four statements largely summarize this epistle, which has been characterized as the fullest expression of Paul's experimental knowledge of Christ. The service of Christ, the humility of Christ, progress toward the perfection of Christ, the invincible power of Christ— for Paul this was the sum and substance of life.

This divine power he is here describing as he declares, "I can do all things," or more literally, "I have strength for all things." This strength comes from Christ. It is imparted to Paul because he is "in Christ," as he states, "in him that strengtheneth me," or "in him that empowers me," or "in him that infuses strength in me." Not only can Paul be independent of material comforts but he can do all things by the power of Christ. "All things" must refer to the purposes of Christ, the will of Christ, the service of Christ; for Paul lives "in Christ." Paul is not granted power for the gratification of his own desires or the accomplishment of any selfish plans; but whatever Christ wishes Paul to do, he grants Paul power to do.

The particular manifestation of divine power to which Paul has been referring is his contentment in the presence of hunger and want. However, Paul would not have his readers infer that their gift has been superfluous, or has not been gladly welcomed. He at once repeats his expression of gratitude and thanks: "Howbeit ye did well that ye had fellowship with my affliction." His need has been very real. His appreciation is hearty and sincere. He says in effect, "It was very kind of you," or "I thank you," or "You did nobly to make common cause, to go shares, with my affliction." By their gift they have become partners of his distress.

In this practical cooperation in missionary work, Paul assigns to the Philippians the very first place. He emphasizes his appreciation and his thanks by recalling the fact that their church had been the only one to give him financial aid in those early days, some ten years before, when he had visited Philippi and had founded the church. As he left them, and during his stay in the neighboring city of Thessalonica, they had cheered and aided him by their generous help: "And ye yourselves also know, ye Philippians, that in the beginning of the gospel, when I departed from Macedonia, no church had fellowship with me in the matter of giving and receiving but ye only; for even in

Thessalonica ye sent once and again unto my need."

It is apparently not drawing too far upon the imagination to trace through this passage a half-playful use of figures drawn from commercial life. By their contributions to him the Philippians have "formed a partnership"; they have "opened an account"; there is a "debit and credit page" in this "matter of giving and receiving."

However, he does not wish his readers to suppose that he is concerned chiefly with his own profit from this partnership. He rejoices in their gift chiefly because they have gained spiritually by their giving. It has been a real benefit to them. They have really been enriched by their transactions. "Not that I seek for the gift," he continues; "but I seek for the fruit that increaseth to your account." Probably the financial metaphor is still in his mind and Paul is saying, "It is not your contribution which concerns me most, but the interest that accrues to your account from this investment."

If Paul is continuing this figure of financial terms, his next phrase may be rendered, not simply, "I have all things, and abound," but, "I am paid in full, and am affluent." When this is connected with what follows, Paul may be said to have here written playfully a formal receipt: "Paid in full; received from Epaphroditus." So, at least, his words may be rendered.

However, their gifts have been no mercenary investment, no mere financial venture. Far from it. They have been made sacred as gifts of love; even more, they have furthered the work of the gospel and have really been offerings to God. God has recognized them; he, and not only his apostle, has been pleased with them. Paul has been satisfied and gratified, but the gifts have been like the fragrance of sweet incense rising to heaven: "I am filled, having received from Epaphroditus the things that came from you, an odor of a sweet smell, a sacrifice acceptable, well-pleasing to God."

In these beautiful terms Paul acknowledges their gifts.

They have relieved his necessity; they have gladdened his heart; they have spiritually enriched the givers; they have pleased God. No wonder Paul can add confidently, "And my God shall supply every need of yours according to his riches in glory in Christ Jesus." God's treatment of them is sure to correspond with their treatment of Paul. They had met all his wants; so God, in his gracious recognition and approval of their sacrificial service, will supply every need of theirs. These needs are both temporal and spiritual. Both are certain to be supplied. "My God," writes Paul, "shall supply every need of yours." Paul can call God his God, for he has found in personal experience what God means to him. God has not forgotten Paul in times of distress and want. Surely he will not disappoint these Philippians but will grant them all their needs; the measure of his kindness will be his illimitable "wealth in glory," or his "riches in glory in Christ Jesus." This treasure house is inexhaustible and as boundless as his infinite love and grace.

These blessings will be enjoyed by the Philippians because of their relation to Christ Jesus and in view of their being in him, or, as some understand the expression, their needs will be supplied according to the riches of grace now revealed "in Christ Jesus" and to be realized fully at his coming in glory.

The very mention of these divine blessings leads Paul to break forth in an ascription of praise: "Now unto our God and Father be the glory for ever and ever. Amen."

IX
THE CONCLUSION
Ch. 4:21-23

21 Salute every saint in Christ Jesus. The brethren that are with me salute you. 22 All the saints salute you, especially they that are of Cæsar's household.

23 The grace of the Lord Jesus Christ be with your spirit.

The doxology which Paul has penned might seem to be a fitting close for his epistle. However, as is his usual practice, he brings his letter to a conclusion by a series of salutations and a benediction. The former are brief, and suited to the character of this informal and friendly communication. It has been conjectured that these last lines may have been written by the apostle's own hand, and not dictated to a scribe or secretary as was probably true of the rest of the letter.

"Salute every saint in Christ Jesus," is equivalent to saying, "Give my Christian greetings to every member of the church," for the word "saint," as will be remembered, was the usual designation of a believer. Nevertheless, the term was a continual reminder of exalted privilege and of obligation to holy living.

The phrase "In Christ" appears to be united here with the word "salute" rather than with the word "saint." Either connection would give a satisfactory meaning. The latter would make the salutation equivalent to, "Remember me to all my fellow Christians." The former would imply, "Extend my greetings in Christ to every believer."

The second salutation, "The brethren that are with me salute you," probably refers to Paul's companions and fellow travelers, and also to those workers who have aided

Paul by preaching the gospel in Rome. The third salutation includes all the members of the church: "All the saints
salute you." These salutations, employing the terms
"saints" and "brethren," with their beautiful implications,
are so familiar as to have become almost commonplace;
but a phrase is added to the last salutation which is surprising, and has occasioned much comment and debate,
namely the words, "Especially they that are of Cæsar's
household." It is not the imperial family, composed of
princes and nobles, but the servants and retainers of the
emperor, which are described by the term "Cæsar's household." This vast establishment of slaves and freedmen
and soldiers formed a considerable fraction of the popula-
tion not only in Rome but also in Italy and the provinces.
More particularly, however, this "household" refers to
such servants as were connected with the imperial palace.

Why they are singled out by the apostle as those who
"especially" desire to be remembered to the Christians
at Philippi one can only conjecture. It would appear that
some of them were well known to these Philippian believers, and might themselves have visited the Macedonian
"colony." On the other hand, Paul may now have been
imprisoned near the palace and have become closely acquainted with the Christian converts belonging to the imperial household. He may, indeed, personally have led to
Christ these servants of the emperor, and mentions them
here as important members of the Roman church.

In any case it is significant to note that there were Christians in "Cæsar's household." That was one of the last
circles where "saints" might be supposed to have been
found. The emperor was Nero, a tyrant whose name is
almost a synonym for profligacy and cruelty. What his
"household" was like, it would not be difficult to imagine.
Yet amid all its darkness and superstition and wicked-
ness the gospel of Christ had taken root and produced a
rich fruitage. There are no conditions over which the
power of Christ cannot triumph. Spiritual life is not devel-

oped so easily in some circumstances as in others, but it can be produced and enjoyed even in the court of a pagan emperor.

To find saints in Caesar's household may be surprising, yet it should also be remarked that this was the very place where saints were most needed. Where heathenism and godlessness are most firmly entrenched, there the true apostle is most eager to have the gospel proclaimed. Where the world is at its worst, there the church should be at its best. The most able messengers should be sent to those regions where the night is still darkest. The very picture of Paul, the prisoner, sending greetings from Caesar's household is a matchless appeal for sacrificial missionary effort.

Again, it may be remarked that Caesar's household might prove to be a center of unusual influence. Loyal witnesses there might mean more for the cause of Christ than in any other circle of the Imperial City. It is wise strategy to bring influence to bear on those centers from which power will be most widely distributed. It is impossible to refrain from allowing fancy to play upon this fact of the saints in the household of Nero, and from imagining what their testimony meant toward the evangelization of the world. For many of these saints their loyal testimony probably meant the arena, the wild beasts, torture, and death; but their immortal memory is enshrined in the heart of the Christian church, because of this salutation that they sent to the saints in Philippi, and their names, too, are written "in the book of life."

In the days of Paul it was customary to close a letter with the single word, "Farewell." The apostle, however, always closes with a benediction. It appears in its simplest form in the epistle to the Colossians: "Grace be with you." In the fullest form "the apostolic benediction" appears at the close of the second letter to the Corinthians: "The grace of the Lord Jesus Christ, and the love of God, and the communion of the Holy Spirit, be with you." In closing his epistle to the Philippians, as, similarly, in the epistles to Philemon and to the Galatians, Paul employs as his closing formula, "The grace of the [or "our"] Lord Jesus Christ be with your spirit."

The essential term is "grace." It is this unmerited favor of God, manifested in Christ Jesus, which has been the determining influence in Paul's own career. In grace God laid hold of Paul when he was on his way to Damascus and transformed him from a persecutor into an apostle. Grace has impelled him to strive continually for moral progress. Grace has enabled him to sing songs in the night, and in the darkness of his Roman imprisonment to write to the Philippians this epistle of joy.

He can breathe no better prayer for these loyal friends than that the grace of God, revealed in Christ Jesus, may be multiplied toward them. He is asking and yearning that by this divine grace their "spirit" may be enriched. "Be with your spirit," is his expression. We might have expected the words "With your spirits." The meaning would have been much the same. However, it is possible that he here is regarding them rightly as being of "one spirit," which indeed is his ardent desire for the church where unity has been in some degree endangered. He is praying that their common and united spiritual life may be enriched. This will be possible by the grace of God. This will be effected by the indwelling Spirit of God. This will redound to the glory of the divine Son of God, "the Lord Jesus Christ."